GRADE **2**

S0-ART-883

ENGAGE THE BRAIN GAMES

MARCIA L. TATE

CORWIN PRESS
Classroom

For information:

Corwin Press
A SAGE Company
2455 Teller Road
Thousand Oaks, California 91320
CorwinPress.com

SAGE, Ltd.
1 Oliver's Yard
55 City Road
London EC1Y 1SP
United Kingdom

SAGE India Pvt. Ltd.
B 1/I 1 Mohan Cooperative
Industrial Area
Mathura Road, New Delhi
India 110 044

SAGE Asia-Pacific Pvt. Ltd.
33 Pekin Street #02-01
Far East Square
Singapore 048763

Printed in the United States of America.

ISBN: 978-1-4129-5931-5

This book is printed on acid-free paper.

08 09 10 11 12 10 9 8 7 6 5 4 3 2 1

Executive Editor: Kathleen Hex
Managing Developmental Editor: Christine Hood
Editorial Assistant: Anne O'Dell
Developmental Writer: Sally Cardoza Griffith
Developmental Editor: Karen Trayser
Proofreader: Mary Barbosa
Art Director: Anthony D. Paular
Design Project Manager: Jeffrey Stith
Cover Designers: Lisa Miller and Monique Hahn
Illustrator: Jenny Campbell
Design Consultant: The Development Source

GRADE 2

TABLE OF CONTENTS

Connections to Standards

This chart shows the national academic standards covered in each chapter.

LANGUAGE ARTS	Standards are covered on pages
Apply a wide range of strategies to comprehend, interpret, evaluate, and appreciate texts. Draw on prior experience, interactions with other readers and writers, knowledge of word meaning and of other texts, word identification strategies, and understanding of textual features (e.g., sound-letter correspondence, sentence structure, context, graphics).	25, 28
Adjust the use of spoken, written, and visual language (e.g., conventions, style, vocabulary) to communicate effectively with a variety of audiences and for different purposes.	14
Apply knowledge of language structure, language conventions (e.g., spelling and punctuation), media techniques, figurative language, and genre to create, critique, and discuss print and nonprint texts.	9, 21, 23, 30
Use spoken, written, and visual language to accomplish a purpose (e.g., for learning, enjoyment, persuasion, and the exchange of information).	17

MATHEMATICS	Standards are covered on pages
Number and Operations—Understand numbers, ways of representing numbers, relationships among numbers, and number systems.	33, 35, 39
Number and Operations—Understand meanings of operations and how they relate to one another.	42
Number and Operations—Compute fluently and make reasonable estimates.	45
Geometry—Analyze characteristics and properties of two- and three-dimensional geometric shapes, and develop mathematical arguments about geometric relationships.	51, 54
Measurement—Understand measurable attributes of objects and the units, systems, and processes of measurement.	48

SCIENCE	Standards are covered on pages
Physical Science—Understand properties of objects and materials.	59
Physical Science—Understand position and motion of objects.	64, 66
Life Science—Understand characteristics of organisms.	61, 70
Earth and Space Science—Understand properties of earth materials.	56

SOCIAL STUDIES	Standards are covered on pages
Understand the ways human beings view themselves in and over time.	83
Understand the interactions among people, places, and environments.	74, 78
Understand individual development and identity.	82
Understand how people organize for the production, distribution, and consumption of goods and services.	81
Understand global connections and interdependence.	85

Introduction

An ancient Chinese proverb claims: "Tell me, I forget. Show me, I remember. Involve me, I understand." This timeless saying insinuates what all educators should know: Unless students are involved and actively engaged in learning, true learning rarely occurs.

The latest brain research reveals that both the right and left hemispheres of the brain should be engaged in the learning process. This is important because the hemispheres talk to one another over the corpus callosum, the structure that connects them.

Using learning games is a valid and important teaching strategy. The mechanisms involved when students are playing a game are just as cognitive as when students are doing math seatwork (Bjorkland & Brown, 1998). Furthermore, play speeds up the brain's maturation process because it involves the built-in processes of challenge, novelty, feedback, coherence, and time (Jensen, 2001).

How to Use This Book

The activities in this book cover the content areas and are designed using strategies that actively engage the brain. They are presented in the way the brain learns best to make sure students get the most out of each lesson: focus activity, modeling, guided practice, check for understanding, independent practice, and closing. Go through each step to ensure that students will be fully engaged in the concept being taught and understand its purpose and meaning.

Each step-by-step activity provides a game that students can use to reinforce learning. Students will enjoy playing variations of classic games such as Pin the Tail on the Donkey, Go Fish, Tic-Tac-Toe, tag, relay races, charades, and more!

Games can be lively, fun, and spirited. The little bit of extra effort it takes to implement games into your curriculum will reap loads in student involvement. Because games can create lots of excitement and healthy rivalry, make sure to set firm ground rules before playing any classroom game.

These brain-compatible activities are sure to engage and motivate every student's brain in your classroom! Watch students progress from passive to active learners as they process competitive, exciting games into learning that is not only fun but also remembered for a lifetime.

Put It Into Practice

L ecture and repetitive worksheets have long been the traditional method of delivering knowledge and reinforcing learning. While some higher-achieving students may engage in this type of learning, educators now know that actively engaging students' brains is not a luxury, but a necessity if students are truly to acquire and retain content, not only for tests but for life.

The 1990s were dubbed the Decade of the Brain because millions of dollars were spent on brain research. Educators today should know more about how students learn than ever before. Learning styles theories that call for student engagement have been proposed for decades, as evidenced by research such as Howard Gardner's theory of multiple intelligences (1983), Bernice McCarthy's 4MAT Model (1990), and VAKT (visual, auditory, kinesthetic, tactile) learning styles theories.

I have identified 20 strategies that, according to brain research and learning styles theories, appear to correlate with the way the brain learns best. I have observed hundreds of teachers—regular education, special education, and gifted. Regardless of the classification or grade level of the students, exemplary teachers consistently use these 20 strategies to deliver memorable classroom instruction and help their students understand and retain vast amounts of content.

These 20 brain-based instructional strategies include the following:

1. Brainstorming and Discussion

2. Drawing and Artwork

3. Field Trips

4. Games

5. Graphic Organizers, Semantic Maps, and Word Webs

6. Humor

7. Manipulatives, Experiments, Labs, and Models

8. Metaphors, Analogies, and Similes

9. Mnemonic Devices

10. Movement

11. Music, Rhythm, Rhyme, and Rap

12. Project-based and Problem-based Instruction

13. Reciprocal Teaching and Cooperative Learning

14. Role Play, Drama, Pantomime, Charades

15. Storytelling

16. Technology

17. Visualization and Guided Imagery

18. Visuals

19. Work Study and Apprenticeships

20. Writing and Journals

This book features Instructional Strategy 4: Games. Through play, people fulfill the body's need to express emotions, to bond with others socially, and to explore new learning with challenge, feedback, and success (Beyers, 1998). In addition, when students are given the opportunity to redesign a game with which they are already familiar, such as Go Fish, Follow the Leader, or Bingo, brain connections are made for a better understanding of the alternate content (Jensen, 1995).

Games involve active learning. They motivate students by making learning fun and engaging. In today's fast-paced world, students are frequently asked to change gears quickly, jumping from one activity to another, sometimes with little time in between to process what they have learned. Using games as a teaching strategy makes sense. Students thrive on the novelty of game playing and the quick action often associated with games. Playing learning games allows students to actively rehearse information they are expected to know in a non-threatening atmosphere. Furthermore, when students are involved in the design and construction of a learning game, the game's effectiveness is enhanced (Wolfe, 2001).

Types of effective learning games include board games, card games, memory games, trivia games, games that encourage physicality, games that involve using the senses, games that involve creative imagination, and many more.

These memorable strategies help students make sense of learning by focusing on the ways the brain learns best. Fully supported by the latest brain research, the games presented in this resource provide the tools you need to boost motivation, energy, and most important, the academic achievement of your students.

CHAPTER 1

Language Arts

Pin the Tail on the Donkey

Objective

Students will add the correct plural endings (-s, -es, -ies) to singular nouns.

Party games can be used in the classroom, even if there is no time for cake and ice cream! In this classic Pin the Tail on the Donkey game, students will practice adding plural endings to singular nouns, giving them a fun and familiar way to learn and practice basic grammar skills.

1. Ahead of time, make a transparency of the **Donkey Pattern reproducible (page 12)**. Tape two large pieces of butcher paper on a wall. Project the transparency image onto each paper and trace the donkey.

2. Create game cards by writing common singular nouns on sentence strips. Write each word on two strips. Cut the strips to fit the words, but leave a blank space at the end so that the "tail" card has a place to go. See the list of suggested words in the box.

Materials
• Donkey Pattern reproducible
• Tail Endings reproducible
• overhead projector and transparency
• tape
• butcher paper
• construction paper or cardstock
• sentence strips
• scissors
• beanbag

-s endings	**-es endings**	**-ies endings**
desks	glasses	pennies
balloons	lunches	cities
drums	boxes	stories
clocks	wishes	parties
numbers	matches	babies
pencils	kisses	countries
kittens	foxes	cherries
homes	beaches	bunnies
sharks	dishes	puppies
friends	branches	kitties
coins	dresses	skies

3. Use the **Tail Endings reproducible (page 13)** to make six construction paper or cardstock tails, three for each team.

4. Before introducing the game, focus students' attention on what they know about adding plural endings to singular nouns. Toss a beanbag back and forth to students as you ask and they answer these questions:
   - *How do we make the singular noun **book** into a plural noun?*
   - *How do we make the word **box** into a plural noun?*
   - *How do we make the word **donkey** into a plural noun?*
   - *How do we make the word **library** into a plural noun?*

5. Tell students they will play a game in which they turn singular nouns into plural nouns. Divide the class into two teams. Give each team a set of "tails" with tape.

6. Attach the donkeys to the wall at a level where students can easily reach them. (Make sure the donkeys' hind ends are facing right so the words and tails can be read from left to right.) Attach the same word card to the hind end of both donkeys.

978-1-4129-5931-5

7. Then model and explain the rules of the game.

    a. When you say: *Pin the tail on the donkey*, both teams read aloud the singular noun.

    b. The first player on each team races to find the tail that has the correct plural ending. Each player pins the tail on the word card.

    c. All team members read aloud the plural noun. The first team to read the correct ending wins a point.

    d. Display a new pair of word cards to continue the game.

8. Play a practice round to make sure students understand how to play the game. Assist students as needed and answer any questions.

9. As a follow-up, have students suggest nouns for more rounds of the game.

Extended Learning

Distribute the word cards to half of the students and the corresponding tails to the other half. Challenge students with singular noun cards to find students with the correct plural endings.

Donkey Pattern

Reproducible 978-1-4129-5931-5 • © Corwin Press

Tail Endings

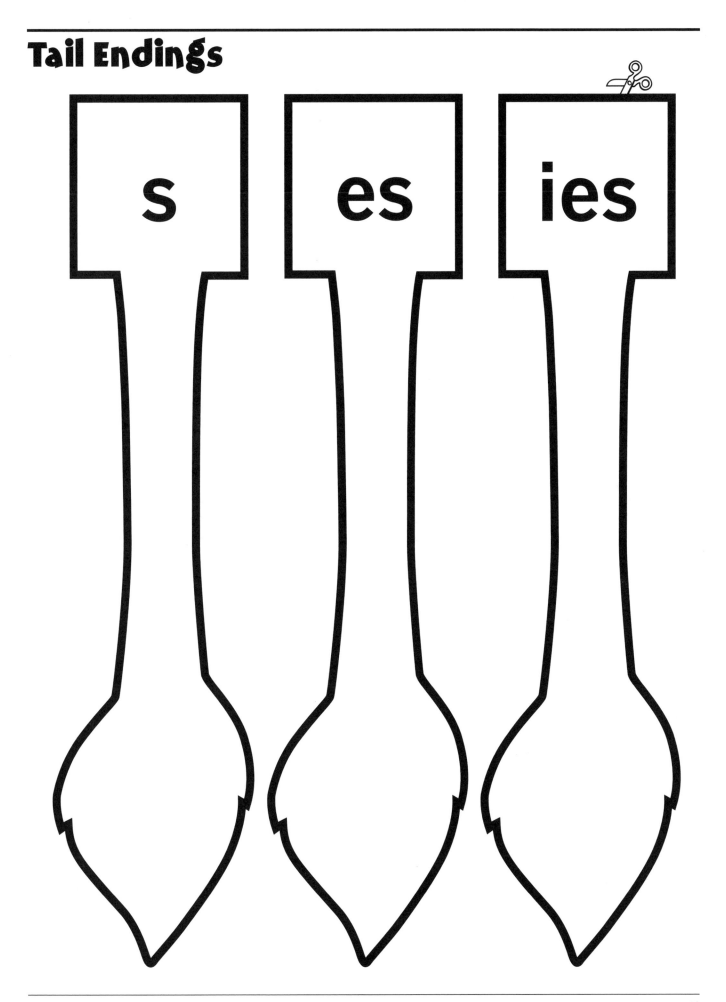

Antonym or Synonym?

Materials
- Antonyms and Synonyms reproducible
- index cards
- 2 containers (e.g., hats, bags, bowls)
- pocket chart
- thesaurus (optional)

Objective
Students will name antonyms and synonyms for given words.

All teachers know the trick of turning off the lights to get students' attention (usually when the class is too noisy). This time, turn off the lights to focus students' attention on a new game that engages their brains in thinking about antonyms and synonyms. In this game, challenge them to become human thesauruses!

1. Ahead of time, copy all of the words from the **Antonyms and Synonyms reproducible (page 16)** onto index cards, or use your own words. Place the word cards in a container. Write *antonym* on seven index cards and *synonym* on seven index cards. Place these cards in another container.

2. Introduce the game by turning off the lights. Ask students: *Who can tell me the antonym for **dark***? When a student answers *light*, turn on the lights with a big *ta-da!* Then tell students they are going to play a game that "turns on" their brain power!

3. Divide the class into teams of six or seven students. Seat students in chairs around a team table or in a team circle. Invite each team to create a team name, and write the names on the board.

4. Explain and model the rules of the game.
   a. Draw a card from the container, read aloud the word (either *synonym* or *antonym*), and place it in a pocket chart. Then draw a word card, read it aloud, and place it next to the first card.
   b. Team members discuss the word and think of either a synonym or an antonym (depending on which card was drawn).
   c. Once a team knows a word, one player stands up. The first player standing provides a synonym or an antonym for the given word.
   d. Write the word on an index card and place it in the pocket chart. (It may be helpful to have a thesaurus.)
   e. If the player gives a correct response, the team earns one point. If the player gives an incorrect response, no point is awarded and the other team has a chance to answer.
   f. Continue the game by drawing a new antonym or synonym card from the container and reading aloud a new word card.
   g. Play continues until all the antonym and synonym cards have been drawn. The team with the most points wins the game.

5. Say a word, and invite students to name both a synonym and an antonym for the word. Repeat with other words to check for understanding. Then begin the game.

6. As a follow-up, discuss some of the antonyms or synonyms. Sort the words into two categories: harder and easier. Discuss why some antonyms and some synonyms are more difficult than others. This activity encourages students to engage in thinking about how they think.

Extended Learning

- Have students make antonym and synonym word cards that are related to their social studies, science, or reading texts.

- Invite students to play a variation of the game. Say a word and its antonym or synonym. Then challenge students to identify the two words as antonyms or synonyms.

Antonyms and Synonyms

Word	Antonym	Synonym
happy	sad	cheerful
dry	wet	arid
opponent	friend	enemy
silent	noisy	quiet
alike	different	similar
dirty	clean	filthy
liquid	solid	fluid
rough	smooth	jagged
respect	insult	honor
problem	solution	question
outstanding	ordinary	superior
forget	remember	overlook
sickness	health	illness
conserve	waste	save
poor	rich	penniless
civil	rude	polite
late	early	tardy
work	relax	toil
hurry	dawdle	rush
morning	evening	daybreak
dangerous	safe	hazardous
master	servant	leader
gentle	violent	calm
past	future	yesterday
defend	attack	protect
lie	truth	falsehood
begin	end	start
long	short	lengthy
different	same	varied
close	open	shut
find	lose	locate
leave	arrive	depart
fix	break	repair
buy	sell	purchase
easy	hard	simple
shy	bold	timid
weak	strong	frail
baby	adult	infant
forgive	blame	excuse

Cause and Effect Charades

Objective

Students will describe the cause and effect of a pantomimed situation.

Cause and effect is a comprehension strategy that students must learn in order to better their understanding of literature. The concept of cause and effect encourages students to consider why something happened and the effect of what happened, which applies to all areas of the curriculum. In this fun game of charades, students act out scenarios that demonstrate cause and effect.

Materials
- Cause and Effect Charades Cards reproducibles
- balloon
- nail

1. Introduce the concept of cause and effect by showing students a deflated balloon. Then blow up the balloon. Ask: *What happened to the balloon?* Discuss how the balloon became bigger because you blew air into it. Then say: *So, the effect of my blowing air into the balloon was that it got bigger. The cause of why it got bigger is that I blew air into it.*

2. Display a nail and ask: *What will be the effect of this nail touching the balloon?* Pull the nail back several times before actually popping the balloon, saying: *Here comes the cause, here comes the cause, the nail is the cause.* BAM! Hold up the deflated balloon and say: *And here is the effect.*

3. Tell students they will play a game of charades to learn more about cause and effect. Divide the class into two teams. Have each team form pairs or trios, depending on the number of students specified on each game card. Give each pair or trio a game card from the **Cause and Effect Charades Cards reproducibles (pages 19–20)**. Read the description of the scenario to students.

4. Invite two or three students to model how to play the game while you explain the rules.
   a. Players read their game card and discuss how to act out the scenario. Players cannot talk during the charade.
   b. Players silently act out the scenario while their teammates watch. No hinting is allowed!
   c. Teammates try to guess the cause and effect of the charade. (It is easier if they say the effect first, then the cause, such as *He fell down because he slipped on a banana peel.*)

d. If the team guesses correctly, they earn two points. If they are not correct, the other team gets a chance to guess and win two points.

e. The game ends when all the charades cards have been used. The team with the most points wins.

5. Invite the class to identify the cause and effect in the first charade. Answer any questions, and then have students play on their own while you carefully monitor the games. Circulate around the room to answer questions and provide assistance as needed.

6. After the game, discuss with students which charades were easiest to guess and why. Discuss the literature that they are currently reading. Have students identify any cause and effect situations they could act out in a future game.

Extended Learning

Invite students to make their own cause and effect game cards. Have them create their own situations or base the charades on situations in the stories they are reading. Use the cards for a new game of charades!

Cause and Effect Charades Cards

Players: 2 ★ ★

Cause: A person eats a banana and then throws the peel on the ground.

Effect: Another person slips on the banana peel and falls down.

Players: 3 ★ ★ ★

Cause: A person makes a sandwich, sets it down on the table, and walks away. Another person comes in, sees the sandwich, eats it, and then walks away. A dog comes in and sits near the table.

Effect: The first person comes in, sees the sandwich is missing, shakes a finger

Players: 2 ★ ★

Cause: An athlete exercises hard and runs a race.

Effect: A judge puts a gold medal around the athlete's neck.

Players: 3 ★ ★ ★

Cause: A mother points at her watch and tells her child to go to bed. The child nods but continues to play video games.

Effect: The next morning the alarm clock rings. (One player is the alarm clock.) The sleepy child gets up late and ends up running after the school bus.

Players: 2 ★ ★

Cause: Goldilocks comes into the Three Bears' house. She sits in Baby Bear's chair and breaks it.

Effect: Baby Bear comes into the room, sees his broken chair, and begins to cry hysterically.

Players: 3 ★ ★ ★

Cause: Three people are driving cars. All of them are talking on their cell phones.

Effect: The three people crash into each other.

Players: 2 ★ ★

Cause: One person tricks another to spend all of his or her money (empties out pockets) on some "magic beans." The beans are supposed to grow until they reach the sky!

Effect: The person plants the magic beans, and watches and watches, but nothing happens. His or her pockets are still empty.

Cause and Effect Charades Cards

Players: 2 ★ ★
Cause: One child sits on the couch and watches TV all day. Another child is outside riding bikes, playing soccer, and mowing the grass.
Effect: The two children walk side by side. The TV watcher moves slowly and heavily. The active child moves quickly and with energy.

Players: 3 ★ ★ ★
Cause: Two students are not paying attention in class, while a third student is paying attention and taking notes.
Effect: The three students reach up eagerly to get their tests back. The first two look sadly at their test papers, and the third one grins happily.

Players: 2 ★ ★
Cause: In a foot race, the hare runs so fast that he tires and naps. The tortoise just keeps walking.
Effect: The tortoise wins the race with his steady pace.

Players: 2 ★ ★
Cause: A child works hard doing laundry, washing dishes, sweeping the sidewalk, raking the leaves, and taking out the trash.
Effect: The father gives the child some money from his wallet.

Players: 3 ★ ★ ★
Cause: Two children are talking and laughing. A third child looks at them shyly and says, "Hi."
Effect: The two children invite the third child to play with them.

Players: 3 ★ ★ ★
Cause: Two dogs growl over a bone. They are so upset that they bark at each other and ignore the bone.
Effect: A third dog comes over, takes the bone, and trots away.

Players: 2 ★ ★
Cause: A mother is working hard all day baking a cake and wrapping presents. She wipes the sweat from her brow.
Effect: Her child smiles as the mother sings and holds out a birthday cake.

Reproducible   978-1-4129-5931-5 • © Corwin Press

Words-Go-Round

Objective

Students will work as a team to brainstorm nouns, verbs, and adjectives for building interesting sentences.

Get students excited about learning grammar by playing a simple game about the parts of speech. Invite them to accept a challenge: Which team can create the most word cards in a Words-Go-Round?

1. Before introducing the game, review the parts of speech with students. Use "doggy terms" to describe nouns, verbs, and adjectives. Explain that the word *dog* is a noun. If a describing word makes sense in front of the word *dog*, that word is an adjective. If an action word can go after the word *dog*, that word is a verb.

   The hungry dog begs.
   A black dog strolls.
   The huge dog flies.

2. Divide the class into three teams. Give the players on each team the same colored marker.

3. Spread index cards over three tables labeled *Nouns, Verbs,* and *Adjectives.*

4. Explain and model the rules of the game.
   a. When you say *go*, each team runs to a different table. Teams must identify the part of speech for their table and write examples of that part of speech on the index cards. Nouns may be plural or singular, common or proper. Verbs may be all tenses, including present tense, past tense, or present progressive tense.
   b. Players cannot repeat words, so they must talk with each other, collaborate, and pay attention to what their teammates are writing. They can also help their teammates by identifying any words that are not correct.

c. After five minutes, ring the bell. Teams collect their index cards and put a rubber band around them. They then rotate to a new table, and for five minutes they write more words. They rotate one more time to finish the Words-Go-Round.

d. After teams have written words at all three tables, they sort their cards and remove any duplicates.

e. Collect each team's cards and count the number of cards for each part of speech. Discuss why some words might need to be eliminated.

f. The team with the most correct cards is the winner! Name a winner for each part of speech. Then count each team's total number of cards for the grand prize.

5. Have volunteers name examples of each part of speech. Answer any questions, and then begin the game.

6. After the game, discuss with students which parts of speech had the most cards. Was it easier for students to brainstorm nouns, verbs, or adjectives? If you find that the words on the cards are not very inspired, invite students to search through their textbooks or library books for better word choices.

Sentence-Building Buddies

Objective

Students will work together to build sentences that make sense.

Materials
- word cards from Words-Go-Round (pages 21–22)
- index cards
- markers

Second graders must be able to recognize and use correct word order in written sentences. They also should be able to distinguish between complete and incomplete sentences, and identify and correctly use various parts of speech, including nouns and verbs. That is a tall order for your beginning readers and writers! In this game, students can practice these skills by engaging in an entertaining and active, brain-friendly game.

1. Ahead of time, sort the student-generated word cards from the Words-Go-Round game into nouns, verbs, and adjectives. Create some cards for two new groups: articles (*the, a, an*) and ending punctuation marks (periods and exclamation points).

2. Compile a set of cards for every five students in your class. Each set will include one card for each part of speech, an article, and an ending punctuation mark. Once you have all the sets compiled, mix up all the cards.

3. Remind students of the Words-Go-Round game they played, in which they made noun, verb, and adjective cards. Tell them that they will use those cards in a new game.

4. Distribute one card to each student. If you have extra students, then they become the "clue givers." Explain that the clue givers mingle among all of their classmates. When they spot a student looking for a certain kind of card, they can whisper: *The card holder you need is wearing a green shirt* (or something equally mysterious).

5. Explain and model the rules of the game.
   a. When you say *go*, players stand up and circulate around the room, reading their classmates' word cards.
   b. When a "noun" finds a "verb," they grab hands and look for an "adjective," an "article," and ending punctuation (a "period" or an "exclamation point").
   c. Once players find buddies with cards that form a sentence, they call out: *Sentence Buddies!* and sit down together. They then wait for their classmates to form sentences.
   d. After all players find a group of "sentence buddies," invite one group to the board. The student with the article card (or a clue giver) writes the sentence created with his or

her group (e.g., *The fancy lady gallops!*). Sentences must make grammatical sense; however, they may be silly or not necessarily true.

e. The whole class reads the sentence and gives it a thumbs-up or a thumbs-down to indicate if the sentence makes sense or not. If the sentence does not make sense, initiate a discussion as to why. Perhaps another group's sentence does not make sense either, and some card-switching needs to take place.

f. Classmates take turns writing and reading each other's sentences. When everyone has shared their sentences, redistribute the cards and play again!

6. Before beginning the game, let students practice by encouraging several volunteers to display their cards. Ask the class to identify the words and help the students form a sentence. Then invite the class to play the game.

7. As a follow-up, read aloud the sentences on the board, and ask students to improve them by switching nouns, verbs, and adjectives to create more appropriate, though perhaps less fun, sentences. For example:

The fast horse gallops!

The fancy lady giggles.

Extended Learning

Invite students to work as a whole group to improve the sentences even further. Help them add new words to make the sentences more interesting and vivid. For example:

The fast chestnut horse gallops across the beach!

The fancy lady giggles shyly into her hand.

The fancy lady gallops!

Plot for Dollars

Objective

Students will match settings, characters, objects, and events to their story titles.

Can you hum the theme song to the game show *Jeopardy*® (a registered trademark of Jeopardy Productions, Inc. dba Merv Griffin Enterprises Corporation)? Invite students to play a new game in the style of Jeopardy® called Plot for Dollars. The goal is to match the titles of stories to their plot details and earn points for every correct match.

1. Ahead of time, choose five or six stories from your reading program or stories that you have read aloud to students. For each story, make setting, character, object, and event cards. For example, clue cards for *The Three Little Pigs* might include *brick house* (setting); *a lazy pig* (character); *straw, sticks* (objects); and *Then the wolf huffed and puffed* (event). Write the name of the story on the back of each card. Other ideas include:
   - *Cinderella: castle* (setting); *fairy godmother* (character); *glass slipper, carriage* (objects); *She ran from the castle, leaving her slipper behind* (event)
   - *The Fox and the Grapes: vineyard* (setting); *fox* (character); *grapes, fence* (objects); *He jumped and jumped but couldn't reach the grapes* (event)
   - *The Mitten: forest* (setting); *hedgehog* (character); *mitten, snow* (objects); *Nicki dropped his mitten in the snow* (event)

2. Also, make a card for each category (*Settings, Characters, Objects,* and *Events*). It is not necessary to have the same number of cards in each category.

3. Make a dollar card for each clue card. Rank the cards from the easiest to the most difficult to answer and assign a dollar amount to each card. Start with ten dollars and count by tens for each successively difficult card. For example, for the setting card *brick house*, make a dollar card for $10 to show how much that answer is worth.

4. Place the clue cards in a pocket chart, organized by category. Place the dollar amount cards in front of the clue cards, sorted by the least amount to the greatest amount.

5. Spark students' interest by asking: *For $50, who can tell me in which story the wolf dresses like a grandma?* Pass out imaginary money when they answer: *Little Red Riding Hood.*

6. Divide the class into three teams, and give each team a signaling device. Explain and model the rules of the game.

   a. One player from each team steps forward and holds the signaling device. A player from the first team chooses a category and a dollar amount (e.g., *I'll take Objects for $30*). Remove the money card and the clue card, and read aloud the clue.

   b. The three players signal if they know which story matches the clue. Call on the first player to signal. If the answer is correct, give the dollar card to the team, and the player chooses a new category and dollar amount. If the answer is not correct, the other two players have a chance to answer.

   c. Play continues with the player who answers correctly choosing another category and dollar amount. Alternate players after two cards have been used.

   d. The game ends when all the cards have been used. The team with the most "dollars" wins!

7. Play a practice round to make sure students understand how to play. Then begin a real game.

8. Extend the game by challenging teams to compete for extra dollars in a bonus round. Have students summarize one of the stories used in the game.

Extended Learning

Invite students to make their own game cards. Each student can make setting, character, object, and event cards from their favorite stories. (This would be a great center activity.) Make sure they write the name of the book on the back of each clue card. Use the game cards for a new round of Plot for Dollars.

"Go Fish" for the Plot!

Objective

Students will match settings, characters, objects, and events to story titles.

Keep the academic language of *settings, characters, objects*, and *events* alive by reusing the game cards from Plot for Dollars. Reuse the cards in this small-group card game based on Go Fish.

1. Tell students to imagine asking the librarian if he or she has any books about little pigs and wolves. Tell them to continue imagining that he or she answered by saying: *Go fish!* While it is not a satisfactory answer from the librarian, it is perfectly okay for the game they will play.

2. Divide the class into teams of two to four players, depending on the number of game cards you wish to use. The more cards there are, the more students can be in a group. Give each student a sheet of construction paper. Show students how to fold along the long edge to form a rectangle. Staple the edges together to create a card holder. This holder will prevent students from being able to read the backs of each other's cards during the game.

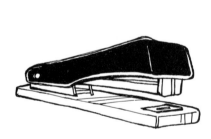 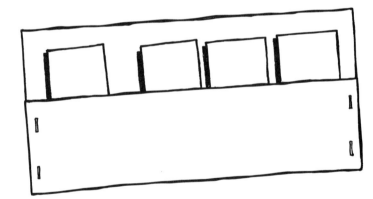

3. Explain and model the rules of the game.
   a. A dealer for each team distributes the game cards, four to each player. Players place their cards in their holder. The dealer places the extra cards facedown in a pile.
   b. The first player looks at his or her cards, identifies any matches, and places those two cards on the table. For example, if the player has *brick house* and *Then the wolf huffed and puffed*, those both match the story *The Three Little Pigs*.
   c. If the first player has no matches, then he or she asks: *Does anyone have a card that matches **brick house**?* (Players must

read the card's clue, not the title of the story.) If another player has a matching card, he or she must give it to the player who asks. (Players only have to give away one card, even if they have more than one card that matches that title.)

    d. If no one has a matching card, the players say: *Go fish for the plot!* That player must then draw a card from the pile. If the card makes a match, the player can lay down the pair and continue the turn. If the card does not make a match, play passes to the player to the right.

    e. Play continues until all the cards have been matched. The player with the most matches wins the game!

4. Have students play a practice round before they play a real game. Circulate around the room to check for understanding and answer any questions.

5. As a follow-up, have students organize each story's cards into a flowchart. Model how to place the setting, character, and events cards in order on a long table. Have students place the object cards under a matching card. (For example, students could put the *straw* card under an event card that reads: *Next, a lazy pig built a weak house*. Invite students to use the cards to retell the story in order.

Extended Learning

Invite students to create a new story by replacing some of the cards in their flowchart with cards for another story. Have them retell their new story to a partner. A new version of *The Three Little Pigs* might end up with the big, bad wolf eating pancakes in a tree house!

"Hang Ten" Guessing Game

Objective

Students will guess letters that form words on their spelling or vocabulary lists from different content areas.

Materials

- index cards
- pocket chart
- paper clips
- individual student chalkboards
- chalk, erasers
- letter or number tiles
- paper lunch bag

Do you remember the old-fashioned game *Hangman*, in which players guessed the letters in a word? This game is similar, except that incorrect answers earn two feet with five toes apiece in the tradition of "hang ten."

1. Ahead of time, make a list of vocabulary or spelling words for which students need extra practice or reinforcement. Choose frequently misspelled words from their writing; vocabulary words from science, social studies, or math texts; and spelling words.

2. Write the alphabet on index cards, one lowercase letter per card. Make the letters as large as possible. Place the alphabet cards in order along the bottom of a pocket chart.

3. Write each game word on an index card. Then write the letters for that word on individual index cards. Paper-clip each word card and its letter cards together.

4. To engage students' attention, act out jumping on a surfboard and "riding the waves." Invite students to join you, and tell them to hang onto the edge of their imaginary boards with their toes. Then draw the "hang ten" symbol on the board, and tell them to get ready to hang ten!

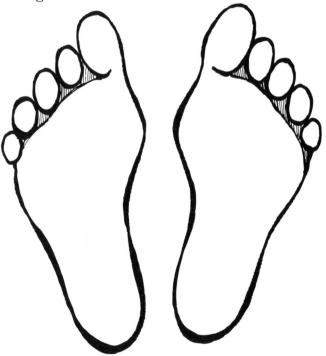

978-1-4129-5931-5

5. Give each student an individual chalkboard, chalk, and an eraser. Explain to the class that they will play a game in which they must identify a word by guessing the letters that form the word. Explain and model the rules of the game.

   a. Place the letter cards for one of the words facedown in the pocket chart. Place the letters from left to right just as you would if players could see the letters.

   b. Have players draw a line for each letter card on their chalkboards.

   c. Give players a clue as to the "category" of the word. For example, name the part of speech or note that the word comes from yesterday's science lesson.

   d. Call on a player to name a letter that he or she thinks is in the word. If the letter is in the word, turn over all the cards for that letter. Players then write those letters on the corresponding lines on their chalkboards.

   e. If the player names a letter that is not in the word, pull that letter card from the alphabet cards and place it at the bottom of the pocket chart. This reminds players not to choose that letter again. Because the letter was not in the word, draw a foot and each successive toe for every letter that is not in the word.

   f. Play continues with a new player naming another letter. The game continues until a player guesses the word or you draw a "hang ten." If a player guesses before you finish drawing "hang ten," he or she wins!

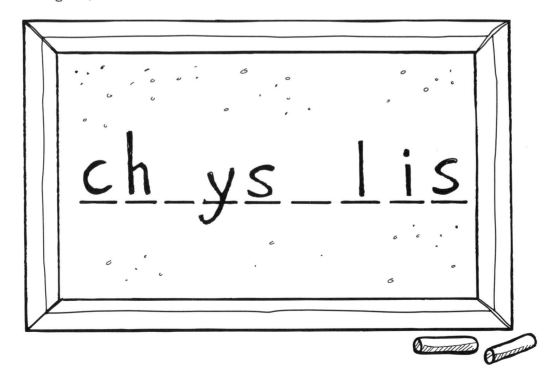

6. Play a practice round to make sure students understand how to play. Then invite them to play a real game. Ask players to draw letter or number tiles out of a bag to determine in which order they guess letters. Players can also compete against each other in pairs or teams.

7. As a follow-up, offer students bonus points if they can correctly use each word in a sentence or define the word.

Extended Learning

Give students an opportunity to make their own word cards. They can then challenge classmates to play the game, while they take turns being the host.

A chrysalis protects the caterpillar as it changes into a butterfly.

CHAPTER 2

Mathematics

Places, Please!

Objective

Students will work together to construct numbers to show correct place value.

Materials
- construction paper
- index cards
- masking tape

Which is the tens place? Which is the hundreds place? Thousands? Where do they go? Sound familiar? Do your second graders get confused when doing place value in math? Rather than complete another worksheet, invite students to play an exciting game to learn about the concept of place value.

1. Ahead of time, number ten pieces of construction paper *0–9*. Make the numbers as large as possible. Make one set of numbers for each team of ten players. Also, draw a large comma on an index card for each team. Use masking tape to create lines on the floor. Use one long piece of tape for each team to show where they will build their number.

2. In order to focus students' thinking, have them stand up and skip-count by tens. When they get to 100, ask them to clap their hands and jump in place. Continue skip-counting by hundreds until you get to 1,000. Have students clap and jump in place some more. Now students should be focused on tens, hundreds, and thousands.

3. Divide the class into teams of ten. Give each team a comma card, and give each team member a number. Explain that students will play a game in which they build numbers together as a team.

4. Explain and model the rules of the game, using one team of volunteers to help you.
   a. Call out a number such as *1,459.*
   b. Players with those numbers race to their starting line and position themselves in the correct place, from left to right.
   c. Once players think they are in the correct positions, another player from the team must place the comma in the correct location.
   d. The team that correctly forms the number first wins a point.

e. If a team forms a number incorrectly, they must reorganize themselves until they are situated correctly.

f. Play continues with you calling out new numbers. The team with the most points at the end of the game wins!

5. Play several practice rounds to check for understanding. Answer any questions students may have. Then play the game.

6. Close the activity by counting by tens to 100 again (to the tune of "Twinkle, Twinkle Little Star"). Challenge teams to form the numbers as quickly as you can sing them! Then challenge them to form numbers from 100 to 1,000 as you skip-count again, singing to the tune of "Happy Birthday."

Pick Your Places

Objective

Students will use number cards to form numbers and show correct place value.

In order to extend the concepts learned in Places, Please! (pages 33–34) and provide students with more individual practice with place value, play an exhilarating game of Pick Your Places. This game works well with small groups or the whole class.

1. Focus students' attention on what they learned in the game *Places, Please!* Tell students that they will play a similar game to learn more about place value.

2. Photocopy enough of the **Pick Your Places Game Cards reproducibles (pages 37–38)** so that each student gets a set. Cut out the cards and place value boxes. Give each student a set of cards in a resealable plastic bag. Tell students to arrange the cards on their desks so the numbers are faceup. Make a transparency of the reproducible, and cut out the number cards and place value box to use for a demonstration.

3. Write a variety of two-, three-, and four-digit numbers on index cards. Include numbers in the ones, tens, hundreds, and thousands places.

4. Give students some practice arranging number cards in the place value box before explaining the game. Tell them to form the numbers *1, 10, 100,* and *1,000.* Use your transparency cards to form the numbers so students can self-correct. Provide more guided practice as needed.

5. Explain and model the rules of the game.
   a. Choose an index card and read aloud the number.
   b. Players use their number cards to form that number in their place value box. The player who finishes first calls out: *Done!*
   c. Check to see if the player's number is correct. If the number is correct, the player gets a point. All players then remove their cards from their place value box and the game continues.
   d. If the number is incorrect, tell the class that it is not correct...yet! If another player called out as well, check his or her answer. If no other player formed the number, continue the game by calling the same number again.

e. The game is over when there are no more number cards. The player with the most points wins!

6. Demonstrate the game with several practice rounds. Call out a number and have volunteers suggest which numbers to place on the transparency. Do this several times and then begin the game.

7. After the game, invite students to use their cards to create the highest number possible (9,999) and the lowest number possible (0). Have students store their game cards in a resealable plastic bag and use them again to play Spin to Win! (pages 39–40).

Extended Learning

Give students addition or subtraction problems that are at their level (e.g., 431 – 265). Invite them to solve the problems and then build the answers in their place value box.

Pick Your Places Game Cards

✂

0	0	0	0
1	1	1	1
2	2	2	2
3	3	3	3
4	4	4	4
5	5	5	5

978-1-4129-5931-5 • © Corwin Press Reproducible

Pick Your Places Game Cards

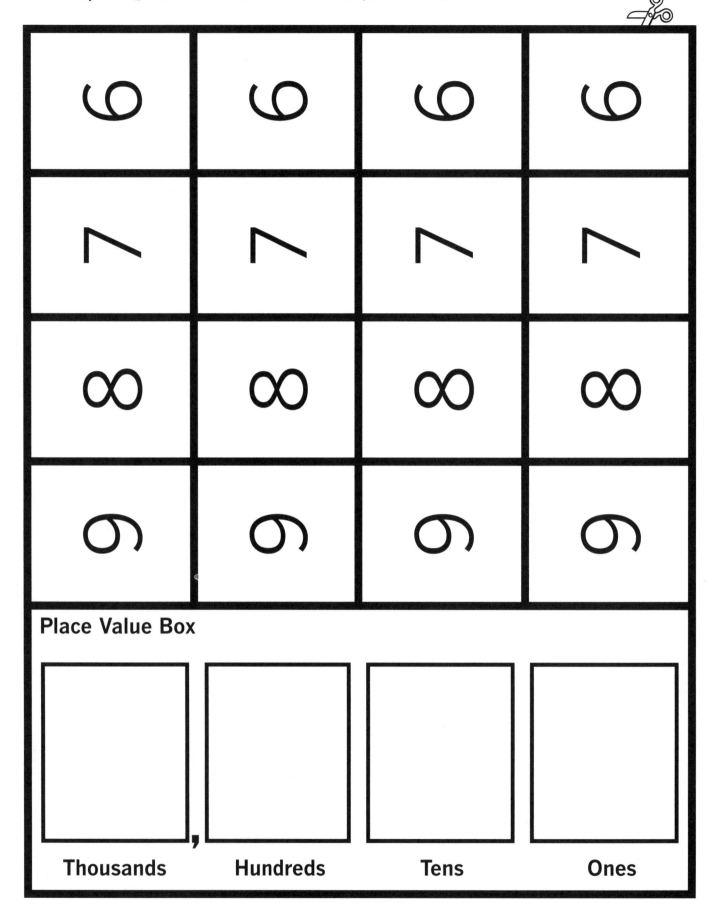

6	6	6	6
7	7	7	7
8	8	8	8
9	9	9	9

Place Value Box

| Thousands | Hundreds | Tens | Ones |

Spin to Win!

Objective

Students will use a spinner and numbers to create number comparisons.

Comparing numbers using the concepts of "greater than" and "less than" is a skill second graders must master to move forward in mathematics. Invite students to play an engaging game of Spin to Win! to make the learning more memorable.

1. To focus students' attention on the concepts of "greater than" and "less than," make a sock into an alligator puppet. Display an assortment of classroom objects, such as a large and a small roll of tape, a large teacher shoe and a small student shoe, and a large and a small book. Hold open the puppet's mouth like the greater than sign (>), and remind students that alligators like to eat big things. Place two objects side by side and invite students to "feed" the alligator. Have volunteers place the larger item in the alligator's mouth.

2. Distribute the number cards and place value boxes that students used in the Pick Your Places game.

3. Divide the class into pairs. Give each pair of students a cardstock copy of a spinner cut from the **Spin to Win! Spinner reproducible (page 41)**, a pencil, and a paper clip. Show them how to place the point of the pencil in one end of the paper clip on the center of the spinner, and flick the paper clip with their finger to spin it.

4. Invite two volunteers to model how to play the game while you explain the rules.
   a. Each player uses number cards to form a number in the place value box.
   b. One player spins the spinner, which will land on *greater than* or *less than*. The player who spins the spinner reads aloud a number sentence that includes both players' numbers and the text on the spinner (e.g., *363 is less than 831*).
   c. If the sentence is true, the player who read the sentence wins a point. If it is not true, the player does not get a point.
   d. Players then form new numbers and the next player spins.
   e. Allow students a set amount of time to play. At the end of the time period, the player with the most points is the winner!

Materials
- Spin to Win! Spinner reproducible
- game cards from Pick Your Places (pages 37–38)
- old sock made into an alligator puppet
- classroom objects of varying sizes
- cardstock
- scissors
- pencils
- large paper clips

5. To check student understanding, write two numbers on the board. Call on a student to hold the sock puppet and "eat" the larger number. Repeat this several times with new numbers and volunteers. Then begin the game. Circulate around the room to check the accuracy of students' number sentences.

6. After the game, ask a volunteer to name a number and challenge classmates to name numbers that are greater than and less than that number.

Extended Learning

Place the number cards in the math center where students can practice with classmates. Students can also take home number sets in resealable plastic bags to practice with a parent or an older sibling.

Spin to Win! Spinner

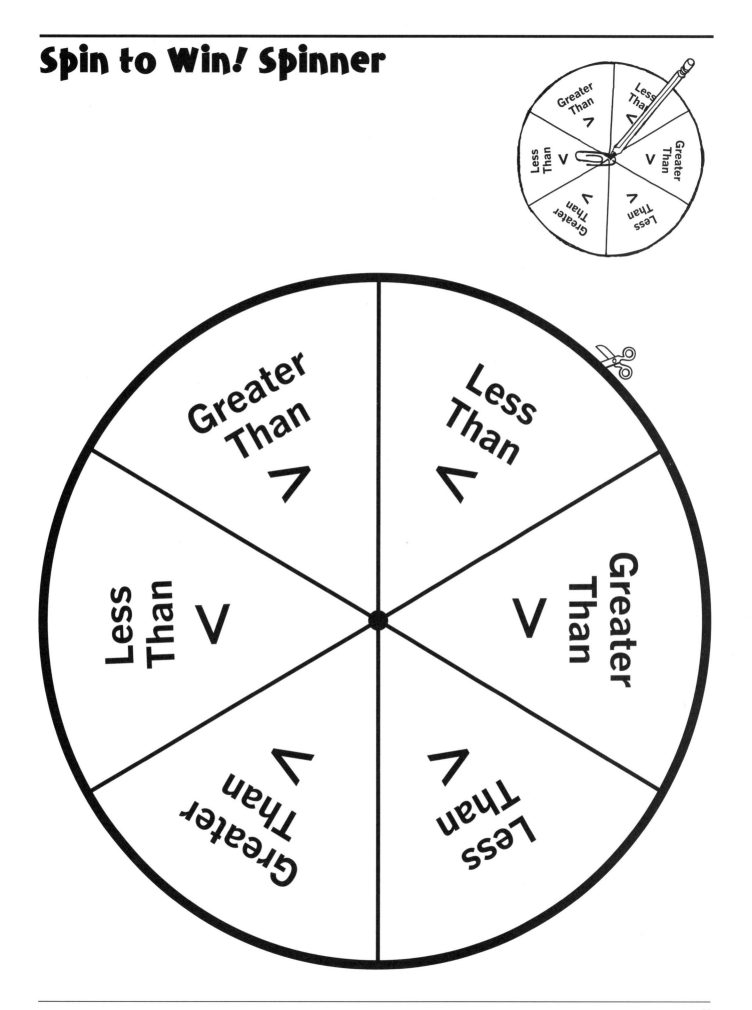

Fact Family Race

Objective

Students will write equations to demonstrate their knowledge of fact families.

In second grade, students must master using the inverse relationships between addition and subtraction to solve problems and check solutions. Playing Fact Family Race provides them with needed practice in using these inverse relationships while competing in a friendly game.

1. Ahead of time, photocopy and laminate a **Fact Family Race reproducible (page 44)** for each student.

2. Bring in pictures of your family to focus students' thinking on fact families. Draw an outline of a house on the board. Write your last name in the roof. Introduce each picture of your family and then tape it in the house. For example, you might say: *This is my son, John Smith, and my daughter, Jane Smith. They live in this house. This is my cat, Spunky Smith. She lives in this house, too!* Then show students a picture of another family. Explain that this family does not live in your house. Draw another house for this family's pictures. Tape the pictures inside the new house.

3. Tell students that numbers can belong in families as well. Numbers in related sentences belong to a fact family, and they can be used to solve problems and check solutions. For example, explain the relationship between $7 + 8 = 15$ and $15 - 8 = 7$.

4. Tell students they will use their knowledge of fact families to play a fast-paced game. Give each student a laminated Fact Family Race reproducible, a washable marker, some facial tissue, and one die or two dice, depending on their ability levels.

5. Display a transparency of the Fact Family Race reproducible, and use it to model how to play the game.
   a. Roll the die and write that number on a blank line on the roof of the house.
   b. Roll the die again and write that number on the second blank line on the roof.
   c. Add together the two numbers and write that number on the blank line at the very top of the house. (If you want students to practice subtraction, then subtract the two numbers and write that number on the third blank line.)

Materials
- Fact Family Race reproducible
- overhead projector and transparency
- family pictures (from home or cut from magazines)
- tape
- washable markers
- facial tissue
- dice

d. Work as quickly as you can to fill out the equations on the rest of the page. Remind students that in addition the big numbers like to go last. But in subtraction the biggest number is the bully and wants to go first!

e. Check your work, thinking aloud. For example, you might say: *Seven plus eight equals 15. Is that true? Yes, it is. So then, eight plus seven equals 15. Hmm, in my subtraction problems, did the biggest number go first? Does 15 take away eight equal seven? Yes, so then 15 take away seven must equal eight.*

6. Once students understand how to set up their game boards, they are ready to play. Have students play in pairs. Explain the following rules:

   a. One player rolls the die or dice to create the number for the first blank line on the roof. Both players write that number on their own roof.

   b. Then the other player rolls the die or dice to create the number for the second blank line on the roof. Both players write that number on their roof.

   c. Players then add or subtract the two roof numbers to get the third number, write it at the top, and then race to fill in the equations. The player who finishes first (with all equations correct) is the winner.

   d. Players clean their game boards and play again with a new set of numbers.

7. Have students play a practice round, and then begin a real game. Circulate to spot-check students' work and answer any questions. Invite them to play several rounds covering a variety of fact families.

8. After the game, have students discuss how they were able to check the accuracy of their equations.

Fact Family Race

Race to 100

Objective

Students will use manipulatives to count in groups of ten to 100.

Race to 100 gives students the opportunity to practice counting by tens to 100, as well as practice changing pennies into dimes and dimes into dollars. These practical, everyday skills are the building blocks for basic math learning.

Materials
- Race to 100 Game Board reproducible
- beanbag
- Unifix® cubes or plastic coins and paper dollars
- dice

1. Toss a beanbag back and forth to students while counting by tens to focus their energy on math. Count by "dimes," too.

2. Then have students play the "hand game" with a partner. Partners slap both of their hands together, clap their own hands, then slap both hands together in a pattern, while reciting the following chant: *One dime is ten cents, two dimes make 20. Three dimes make 30 cents, and four dimes make 40. Five dimes make 50 cents, and six dimes make 60. Seven dimes make 70 cents, and eight dimes make 80. Nine dimes make 90 cents, but ten make a dollar!*

3. Tell students they will play a game to help them count by tens to 100. Divide the class into pairs. Give each pair two copies of the **Race to 100 Game Board reproducible (page 47)**, Unifix cubes or play money, and one die.

4. Invite a volunteer to demonstrate how to play the game with you as you explain the rules.
   a. Player 1 rolls the die. The number rolled tells the player how many Unifix cubes (or pennies) he or she puts on the game board.
   b. Player 2 rolls the die and places Unifix cubes (or pennies) on his or her game board.
   c. Players continue rolling the die and filling up their game boards until one player gets ten cubes or pennies to make a group of ten. (If students are using cubes, have them link the cubes together to make a "ten-stick." If they are using pennies, have them trade ten pennies for a dime.)
   d. Players then start with a clean game board and continue playing. The first player to reach 100 or $1.00 wins!

5. Have partners play a practice round, and then allow students to play on their own. Circulate around the classroom, making sure students understand how to make a dollar from ten dimes or a ten-stick from ten Unifix cubes.

6. After the game, invite students to bring all of their ten-sticks to a circle on the carpet. Ask them to estimate how many individual cubes the class has all together.

7. Then go around the circle. Have each student hold up his or her ten-stick while the whole class counts by tens. Watch students' eyes grow rounder the closer they get to 1,000!

Extended Learning

Have students who are ready for more of a challenge fill up their game boards with dimes. Have them trade ten dimes for a dollar. The player who gets ten dollars first is the winner!

Race to 100 Game Board

It's About Time!

Materials
- It's About Time! Clock reproducible
- construction paper
- scissors
- brads
- index cards

Objective

Students will practice telling time to the hour, half hour, and quarter hour.

In second grade, students need to learn to tell time to the nearest quarter hour. Play this quick, exciting game to make learning to tell time an enjoyable and memorable way for students to practice new math skills.

1. To spark students' interest, invite them to discuss with a partner what time their favorite TV show starts, what time they eat dinner, and what time they go to bed. Listen as they talk, and record the times they say on the board. Invite students to point out the times that show the hour, half hour, and quarter hour. Then, tell them that since they are already experts with time, they get to play a time game.

2. Give each student a construction paper copy of the clock parts from the **It's About Time! Clock reproducible (page 50)**. Show them how to use a pencil to poke a hole through the center and hands of each clock. Have students insert a brad through the hour hand, the minute hand, and the center of the clock. Show them how to open the brad at the back of the clock to secure the pieces in place. Make a clock for yourself as well.

3. Make "time cards" by writing times on index cards. Write times on the hour, half hour, and quarter hour (e.g., *11:45, 4:15, 7:30, 9:00, 8:45, 12:00, 6:15, 2:30*).

4. Divide the class into two teams. Have students sit in chairs in two parallel rows, facing each other, one team in each row. Each student should be holding a clock.

5. Explain and model the rules of the game.
   a. Draw a time card and say the time. Show the matching time on your clock, but don't display the clock to players yet.
   b. Players show the matching time on their clocks but keep the clocks facedown in their laps until you say: *It's about time!* and show your clock.
   c. Players then show their clocks to the opposite team.
   d. Teams earn one point for each player whose clock shows the correct time.
   e. Continue the game by drawing new time cards and challenging players to show the time.

f. The team with the most points at the end of the game wins. Play for a specified amount of time or until the time cards run out.

6. Have students play several practice rounds to check for understanding. Allow them to discuss the correct time, while keeping their clocks hidden from the opposing team's view. Then call out: *It's about time!* Have students show their clocks to the opposing team as you show the correct time on your clock. Then begin a real game.

7. As students play and show incorrect times on their clocks, tally the points but then use that same time card again right away! The students who missed it the first time will have a chance to correct their mistake immediately, providing an excellent opportunity for reinforcement.

8. After the game, invite student to discuss why it is important to be able to tell time. Have them name the things they use to tell time.

Extended Learning

- Place the game materials in the math center for more practice. On the back of each time card, draw a clock that shows the matching time. Ask a student to call out the times to the center group. Players show the time on their clocks, and the caller displays the back of the time card to show the correct time.

- Have students use their clocks to show duration of time as well. Call out a time using the time cards. Have students show that time on their clocks. Then call out a unit of time that has passed (e.g., *four hours later*). Students then move the clock hands to the time that shows four hours have passed.

Name _____   Date _____

It's About Time! Clock

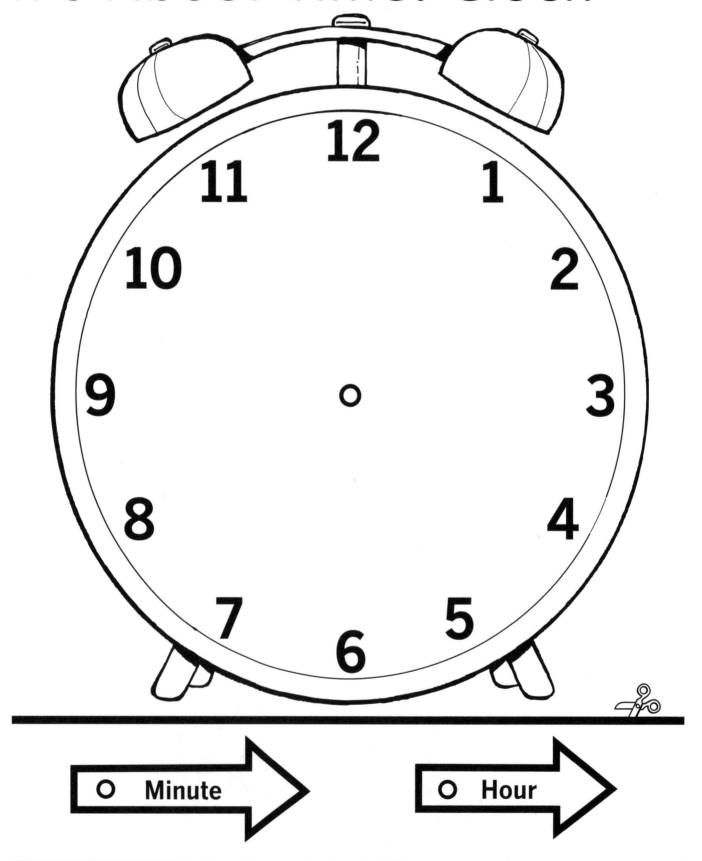

Shape Shifters

Objective

Students will identify the properties of shapes and solid figures.

Materials
- Shape Shifters Riddles reproducible
- game show "buzzers" (e.g., noisemakers, bells, spoons, pie tins)

Shift visual learning into auditory learning by playing the Shape Shifters game. This game allows students to demonstrate their understanding of the characteristics of plane and solid geometric shapes.

1. Focus your classroom toward playing a game about shapes and solids by inviting students to answer a riddle. For example: *What did the hen say when her chick won a prize? Eggstraordinary!* Invite students to share their own riddles. Once students have caught the "riddle spirit," it's time to play Shape Shifters!

2. Divide the class into two or more teams, depending on how many "buzzers" you have. (Each team needs a buzzer.) Make a copy of the **Shape Shifters Riddles reproducible (page 53)** to use for the game. If you wish, write additional riddles of your own, or ask students to work in pairs to write riddles.

3. Explain the rules of the game, and model using several volunteers.
   a. Each team sends a player to the front of the room.
   b. Read aloud a Shape Shifters riddle. Any players who can identify the shape based on the riddle should "buzz in" to signal that they want to answer.
   c. Call on the player who signaled in first. If the player answers correctly, his or her team gets one point. If the player answers incorrectly, the other players have a chance to solve the riddle.
   d. The game ends when all ten riddles have been answered. The team with the most points wins the game!

Eggstraordinary!

4. Invite students to play a practice round with a sample riddle, such as: *What's black and white and red all over? (An embarrassed panda bear, of course!)* Remind students that if they buzz in before the riddle is read completely, then you will stop reading and they must answer the riddle. Explain that their teammates cannot provide clues or help them figure out the answers.

5. As a follow-up, ask students to reflect on which riddle was the most difficult to answer. Discuss what made that riddle so difficult. Then challenge students' memories by reading the riddles again. But this time, invite students to work as a group to form their bodies into the shapes rather than saying the answers.

Extended Learning

Invite students to play a "quick draw" version of the riddle game. Organize teams as you did before. Have one player from each team stand at the chalkboard. In this version of the game, instead of answering a riddle, students must draw the figure being described. The first player to accurately draw the figure wins a point for his or her team.

Shape Shifters Riddles

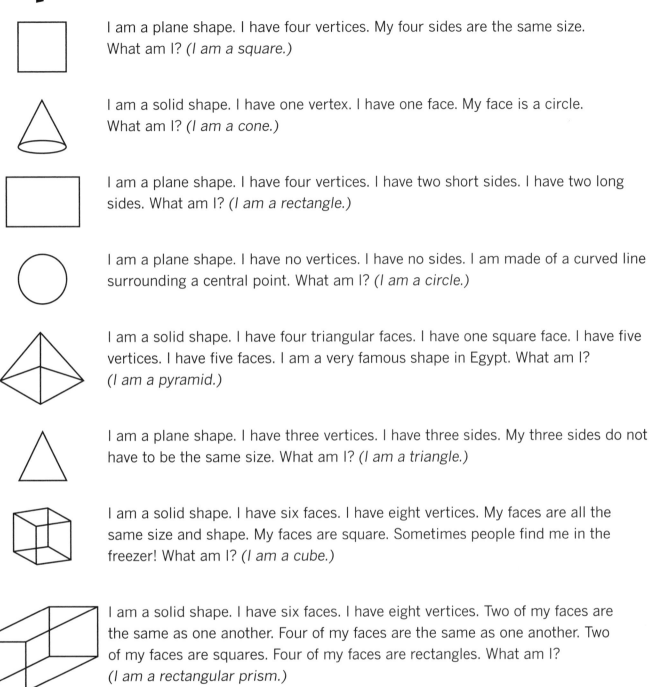

I am a plane shape. I have four vertices. My four sides are the same size. What am I? *(I am a square.)*

I am a solid shape. I have one vertex. I have one face. My face is a circle. What am I? *(I am a cone.)*

I am a plane shape. I have four vertices. I have two short sides. I have two long sides. What am I? *(I am a rectangle.)*

I am a plane shape. I have no vertices. I have no sides. I am made of a curved line surrounding a central point. What am I? *(I am a circle.)*

I am a solid shape. I have four triangular faces. I have one square face. I have five vertices. I have five faces. I am a very famous shape in Egypt. What am I? *(I am a pyramid.)*

I am a plane shape. I have three vertices. I have three sides. My three sides do not have to be the same size. What am I? *(I am a triangle.)*

I am a solid shape. I have six faces. I have eight vertices. My faces are all the same size and shape. My faces are square. Sometimes people find me in the freezer! What am I? *(I am a cube.)*

I am a solid shape. I have six faces. I have eight vertices. Two of my faces are the same as one another. Four of my faces are the same as one another. Two of my faces are squares. Four of my faces are rectangles. What am I? *(I am a rectangular prism.)*

I am a solid shape. I have no sides. I have no vertices. If you cut me in half, my face would be a circle. I am known all around the world! What am I? *(I am a sphere.)*

I am a solid shape. I have five faces. Two of my faces are triangles. Three of my faces are squares or rectangles. I have six vertices. What am I? *(I am a triangular prism.)*

Pattern Partners

<table>
<tr><td>

Materials
• Unifix cubes
• construction paper
• bell

</td></tr>
</table>

Objective

Students will create and extend patterns.

In order to progress to higher-level mathematics concepts, students must learn to recognize and predict patterns. Since the brain loves patterns, this game will be both brain friendly and kid friendly. Students will work to create and extend patterns while playing with cubes.

1. Review different kinds of patterns which the class, such as AB, ABC, AABB, and ABBC. Challenge students to create different hand motions to show the patterns (e.g., snapping and clapping). Be sure that students have a good understanding of a "pattern unit," or the piece of the pattern that repeats.

2. Place piles of Unifix cubes on tables around the room. Then place pieces of construction paper on the tables to create "stations" where students can work. It may be helpful to use different-colored paper to distinguish one station from another. Decide on the order in which students will move from one station to another (e.g., a clockwise rotation).

3. Divide the class into pairs. Then model the game for students while you explain the rules.
   a. Players work with their partner to create a pattern that is two pattern units long.
   b. Partners use the cubes to create their pattern and then place the cubes on the construction paper. Partners write their names on their paper at the first station only.
   c. When partners hear the bell, they rotate to the next station. Players analyze the pattern in one set of cubes and then continue the pattern by adding another pattern unit to it.
   d. Players continue rotating to new stations and extending patterns until they return to the station with their original pattern. At this point, players analyze the extended version of their pattern to see if it is correct. If it is correct, the class gets a point. For every point the class earns, award a prize such as extra recess time, pencils, or stickers.

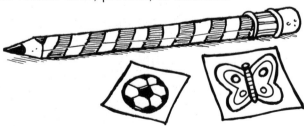

4. Use Unifix cubes to create a pattern. Ask students to identify the pattern. Have a volunteer add cubes to extend the pattern. Do this with several more patterns to make sure that students understand how to play. Then begin the game.

5. Ring the bell about every two minutes. Allow students to move the construction paper station to the floor if they need more room to extend the patterns.

6. After the game, discuss with students which patterns were easier to work on and which were more difficult. If any patterns "went wrong," challenge students to find where the pattern units went awry and then correct it together.

Extended Learning
Have students use crayons or markers to copy their patterns onto sentence strips. Use these strips as a border for your math bulletin board or to line the walls of your classroom!

CHAPTER 3

Science

"Rock Your Memory" Matching Game

Materials

- "Rock Your Memory" Game Cards reproducible
- *Everybody Needs a Rock* by Byrd Baylor
- construction paper
- scissors
- resealable plastic bags

Objective

Students will match words and definitions related to rocks and soils.

Invite your young scientists to explore the properties of rocks and soil and learn about ways that people use these natural resources. To help cement the properties of these materials into students' memories, invite them to play Rock Your Memory, a game played similarly to the popular commercial game *Concentration*® (a registered trademark of NBC Universal, Inc.).

1. Get students thinking about rocks by reading aloud the book *Everybody Needs a Rock* by Byrd Baylor. Then teach students the following chant:

    Let's r-o-c-k, rock. (clap)

    Let's r-o-l-l, roll. (clap)

    Let's roll like a boulder,

    Roll like a large rock, (hands make rolling motion)

    Not like a tiny rock, (shake finger "no")

    Not like a grain of sand!

    Let's r-o-c-k, rock. (clap)

    Let's r-o-l-l, roll. (clap)

    Let's roll like a boulder,

    Roll like a boulder, (roll hands)

    Not like a grain of sand! (shake finger and head "no")

2. Make construction paper copies of the **"Rock Your Memory" Game Cards reproducible (page 58)**, and cut out a set of cards for each student pair. Place each set in a resealable plastic bag.

3. Divide the class into pairs of students. Give each pair one set of cards.

4. Model playing the game with a volunteer as you explain the rules.
    a. Players place the cards facedown in a grid pattern of three cards across and four cards down.

b. The first player turns over two cards. If the player turns over a vocabulary word card that matches a definition card, then the player keeps the two cards.

c. If the two cards do not match, the player gives his or her partner a chance to read them and then turns the cards facedown again in the same position. (It is important that players keep the cards in the same position. That way, the brain has a chance to remember where cards are located.)

d. The second player takes a turn flipping over two cards at a time, and play continues. The challenge is not only making matches, but also remembering where previously turned-over cards are located.

e. After all cards are matched, the player with the most pairs wins the game.

5. Lay out a set of cards and turn over two cards at a time. Read aloud the cards and ask students if they match. Answer any questions, and then have students play on their own.

6. After the game, ask students to discuss how they used their memory while playing the game. Invite them to offer advice and special memory techniques to classmates.

Extended Learning

- Invite students to make their own sets of memory cards using vocabulary words and definitions from other units in science or in other curricular areas. Place the cards at a center and challenge students to play on their own or with a partner.

- Place a variety of rocks in your science center. Ask students to examine and sort the rocks by size, color, shape, texture, and more.

"Rock Your Memory" Game Cards

Boulder	Tiny rock	A hard, nonliving thing that comes from the earth
Large rock	Soil	Grain of sand
Rock	Loose top layer of the earth's surface	Soil that has many bits of dead plants and animals in it
Clay soil	Topsoil	Soil that is made up of tiny pieces of rock that stick together easily

Reproducible

Liquid Tag

Objective

Students will learn about the movement of fluid and viscous liquids.

Materials
- teaspoon
- water, milk, syrup
- glass
- cookie sheet

The study of matter is part of the second-grade science standards. Students learn that a liquid is a form of matter that does not have its own shape. It takes up space and has mass. In this game, students will enjoy learning the concept of fluidity and viscosity as they explore how quickly liquids pour.

1. Ask the class: *Have you ever poured yourself a glass of milk? Can you show me what it looks like to pour a glass of milk? How long does it take until the glass is full?* Then ask: *Have you ever poured yourself a glass of syrup or honey? Can you show me what it would look like? How long does it take until the glass is full?*

2. Introduce students to the concepts of fluid liquids and viscous liquids. Explain that you will demonstrate that fluid liquids flow quickly and viscous liquids flow slowly. Pour a teaspoon of water, milk, and syrup on the top of a cookie sheet. Ask students to shout *go*, and tilt the cookie sheet so the liquids pour down the surface. Explain that the liquid that reaches the bottom first is the most fluid, and the liquid that reaches the bottom last is the most viscous.

3. Invite students to go outside and stand on the end line of a basketball court. Tell them they are going to play Liquid Tag. Explain how to play the game.
   a. Stand by the basketball hoop, shout *fluid*, and then turn away from students.
   b. Players should walk quickly toward you. When you turn around and shout *freeze*, students must stand still.

FLUID!

c. When you shout *viscous* and turn away again, players should slowly walk forward, as if they were moving through syrup. When you turn around and shout *freeze,* students must stand still.

d. Play continues until a player is able to reach out and touch your arm. This student becomes the new leader, and a new game begins.

4. Play a practice round, but do not turn away from students. Monitor them to make sure that their movements match the terms *fluid* and *viscous*. Then begin the game.

5. As a follow-up, ask students to name fluids that move slowly and quickly and identify them as *fluid* or *viscous*.

Extended Learning

Students enjoy racing the liquids themselves! Give a pair of students a cookie sheet covered with a piece of waxed paper, which allows for easy cleanup. Have students first predict which liquid they think will be more fluid or more viscous. Allow them to experiment with different liquids, such as hand soap, shampoo, honey, chocolate milk, corn syrup, and orange juice. Then have students place a teaspoon of each of three liquids at one end of the cookie sheet, tilt the sheet, and watch the liquids race to the bottom. Ask students to record their discoveries and explain which liquid "won" the race and why.

Classify Those Animals

Objective
Students will sort and classify animal characteristics by their animal group.

Second graders learn that scientists observe, sort, and classify animals into groups. The animals in the groups have similar characteristics. In this game, students work together to classify those characteristics into the correct animal groups.

Materials
- Classify Those Animals reproducible
- sentence strips
- chart paper
- glue or tape

1. Engage students' musical intelligence as they focus their attention on animal groups. Sing the following verses to the chorus tune of "Three Blind Mice":

   I'm thinking of a group (two times)
   That includes an alligator. (two times)
   What is it? (two times) *(reptiles)*

   I am thinking of a group (two times)
   Of animals that have feathers. (two times)
   What is it? (two times) *(birds)*

2. Ahead of time, copy the information from the **Classify Those Animals reproducible (page 63)** onto sentence strips. If you wish, create additional sentence strips for the game.

3. Tell students that they will play a game in which they classify animals. Explain and model the rules of the game.

   a. Each player gets a sentence strip that contains information about an animal group. It might be the name of the group, the name of an animal representing that group, or a characteristic of an animal from that group.

   b. When you say *go*, players look for their classification group. For example, the player who has *I am a reptile* must find the player who has a characteristic of a reptile (e.g., *I have scaly, dry skin*).

   c. Then, those two players must find the player who has the matching animal (i.e., *I am a lizard*). When players complete their group, they sit on the carpet. (There are two characteristic cards per animal group and one card of an animal representing each group.)

   d. The first team to sort and classify its animal group wins, but the game is not over yet! The main object of the game is for the whole class to sort the cards and sit down.

e. Once the whole class is sitting, each group presents its information. The player who has the group name card stands up and speaks first (e.g., *This is the reptile group, and I am a reptile*). Then the other cardholders speak (e.g., *I have scaly, dry skin. I am a lizard.*).

f. After each group has presented its cards, ask the class to check for accuracy. Does every card belong to that group? If the class finds a mistake, the player with that card must find and move to the correct group.

4. Read aloud several cards, and ask students to identify which cards go together to form an animal group. Repeat as needed to make sure students understand how to play. Then begin the game.

5. As a follow-up, have students glue or tape their sentence strips onto chart paper. Invite them to draw or attach pictures of animals that belong in each group.

Extended Learning

Challenge individual students to sort and classify. Give students a copy of the Classify Those Animals reproducible. Have them cut out the cards, sort and classify the cards into animal groups, and glue them onto a sheet of construction paper.

Classify Those Animals

I am a mammal.	I am a lizard.	I am a fish.	I have smooth, wet skin.
I have feathers.	I have hair or fur.	I am a parrot.	I have scaly, dry skin.
I drink milk from my mother.	I have six legs.	I am a reptile.	I am an insect.
I am a gorilla.	I am a shark.	I have two antennae.	I have a beak but no teeth.
I use gills to breathe.	I am an amphibian.	I live in water and on land.	I must live in the water.
I am a bird.	I am a dragonfly.	I am a salamander.	I sit in the sun to warm my blood.

The Commotion of Motion (Outdoors)

Materials

- masking tape
- hula hoops
- tennis balls
- jump rope
- small box

Objective

Students will explore the concept of force.

In science, a "force" is a push or a pull that makes something move. The force of moving air is called wind, which is used to push things like sailboats or pinwheels. Gravity is the force that pulls things toward the center of the earth. The force of magnetism attracts, or pulls, objects made of certain metals. Allow students to explore these concepts as they engage in the commotion of motion.

To spark students' curiosity, ask them to chant the nursery rhyme "Jack and Jill." Then ask: *Did Jack use the force of pulling to move the pail of water?* Help students realize that the force of gravity caused Jack and Jill to tumble down the hill. Explain that they will explore the concept of force by playing games outdoors. Model and explain the following games before allowing students to play.

Hula Hoop Push

Take the class to an outdoor play area. Use masking tape to create a starting line. Tell students that the first activity is a hula hoop rolling contest. Challenge students to see who can roll a hula hoop the farthest.

1. Players stand on the starting line. One at a time, they push, or roll, a hula hoop as fast as they can.

2. When the hula hoop falls, the player runs and sits inside of it. Players stay seated until everyone has had a turn. (If you need more hula hoops, just take them from the seated players.)

3. The player seated farthest from the starting line wins!

Students can play a similar game using balls. Have players stand on the starting line and throw, or "push," a ball as hard as they can. The player who throws the ball the farthest is the winner.

Tug-of-War Pull

Use the traditional game of tug-of-war to demonstrate the power of pull.

1. Tie a handkerchief in the middle of a long jump rope. Put a hula hoop on the ground and stretch the jump rope across it, with the handkerchief marking the middle of the rope in the center of the hoop.

2. Divide the class into small teams that can compete against each other, rather than having two large teams.

3. Place one team on each side of the hoop. When you say *pull,* the players on each team pull on the rope as hard as they can. The goal is to pull the handkerchief out of the hoop's circle and toward one's own team. The team who accomplishes that task first is the winner.

Box Drop

Next, have students experiment with the force of gravity. Place a hula hoop at the bottom of a slide. Explain that students will have to use gravity to help them win the game.

1. One player climbs to the top of the slide. Hand the player a small box.

2. The player places the box on the top of the slide and gives it just enough of a push so it slides down the slide and into the hula hoop. The player who can make the box land inside the hula hoop is the winner!

While students are playing the games, circulate around the play area to make sure they are playing by the rules and displaying good sportsmanship. Answer any questions and provide assistance as needed.

After the games, invite students to discuss the different forces they used to play each game. Invite them to tell which game they enjoyed most.

The Commotion of Motion (Indoors)

Materials
- Paper Clip Chase reproducible
- rulers
- marbles
- empty, clean gallon milk jug
- clothespins
- bar magnets
- large paper clips

Objective
Students will explore the concept of force.

Continue your exploration of physical science inside the classroom, focusing on the concept of force. Inside, the "commotion of motion" becomes much more obvious. Move the desks back to give students a lot of floor space as they get ready to investigate the forces of pushing and pulling.

Focus students' attention on forces by asking them to describe how they moved their hula hoops from one place to another when they played outside (see The Commotion of Motion [Outdoors], pages 64–65). Students will tell how they used their arms, torsos, and legs to push the hula hoops as hard as they could. Explain that in the classroom, they will not need to exert quite as much force as they did outside. Model and explain the following games before allowing students to play.

Marble Push
Divide the class into pairs. Give each pair a ruler and a marble. Challenge players to see which partner can give the marble the hardest push, as measured by how many inches the marble travels.

1. Have players set the marble next to the zero mark on the ruler, or next to the edge of the ruler.

2. Players cannot touch the marble with their fingers or hands. They must push the marble with their nose.

3. One player pushes the marble once with his or her nose. The other player uses the ruler to measure the distance the marble traveled. Then it's the next player's turn. The player whose marble travels farther is the winner.

Tennis Shoe Pull

This game is for the whole class. Tell students that they will be using their tennis shoes to explore the force of pulling. Point out that less force is needed to move something light than something heavy, even in footwear!

1. One player comes to the front of the room and sits in a chair, with his or her back facing the class.

2. Three other players come quietly to the front of the room and each hand you a shoe. You then hand one of the shoes, by the laces, to the seated player. The other three students take turns saying:
   I am _____, and that is my shoe!

3. The seated player pulls the shoe up and down to feel the force. He or she needs to think about the size of the other players and whose shoe it could be. He or she then makes a guess based on these observations: *I think this shoe belongs to _____!*

4. If the guess is correct, the class gets a point. If the guess is not correct, then you get the point! The first one to get ten points (you or the class) wins the game.

Clothespin Drop

Give students a fun way to explore gravity by challenging them to drop clothespins into a clean gallon milk jug. Divide the class into pairs for this game.

1. One player kneels on a chair, facing the back of the chair, and holds onto the chair back for support.

2. His or her partner places the milk jug behind the chair and hands the first player a clothespin. That player tries to drop ten clothespins into the jug. Then it's the next player's turn.

3. The player who drops the most clothespins into the jug is the winner.

978-1-4129-5931-5

Paper Clip Race

Explain that magnetism is a force that pulls. Challenge students to use magnetism as they compete in a paper clip race. For this game, give each student a copy of the **Paper Clip Race reproducible (page 69)**, a large paper clip, and a bar magnet.

1. Players form pairs or groups of three.

2. Players put a paper clip on the *Start* position on the reproducible. They hold the paper with one hand and hold a magnet under the paper with their other hand. The magnet attracts the paper clip through the paper.

3. Players try to move the paper clip through the path to the finish line. The first player to reach the finish line is the winner.

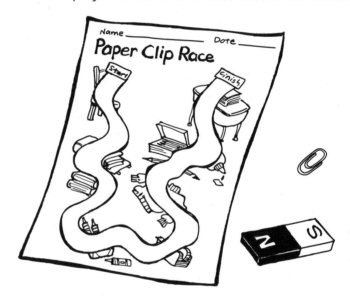

While students are playing the games, circulate around the room to make sure they are playing by the rules and displaying good sportsmanship. Answer any questions and provide assistance as needed.

After the games, discuss with students all of the various ways they explored the concept of force inside and outside of the classroom. Which activities involved pushing, pulling, or gravity? Review the activities and concepts. Ask student which game was their favorite and why.

Extended Learning

Invite students to be aware of everyday activities that involve force, such as pulling open a door, pushing in a drawer, or catching a ball as it falls to the ground. Have students keep a science log in which they record their observations of how force is used in their everyday lives. Once a week, have students compare journals with a partner to help them recognize other activities that involve force.

Paper Clip Race

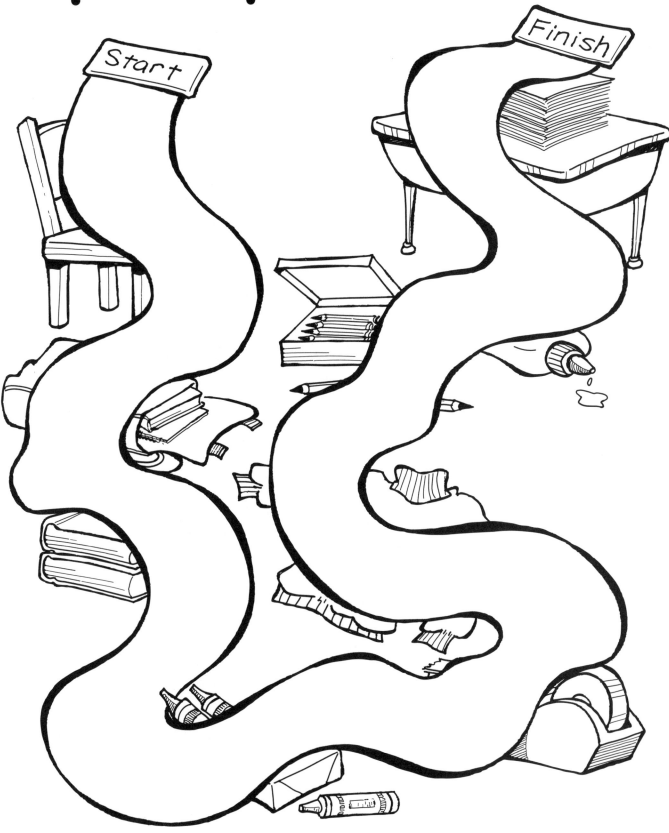

"Pyramid of Fun" Quiz Game

Materials

- Pyramid of Fun: Questions and Answers reproducibles
- pictures of Egyptian pyramids
- butcher paper
- magazines
- scissors
- glue
- squishy ball

Objective

Students will review their knowledge of the body's main systems.

The national science standards dictate that second graders must understand basic information about the digestive, skeletal, muscular, and circulatory systems. The food pyramid is another concept they must learn about. Invite students to play Pyramid of Fun, which gives them practice working with these concepts.

1. Show students pictures of the pyramids in Egypt. Spark their curiosity by asking what a pyramid has in common with their lunch. Then introduce them to the concept of the food pyramid.

2. Use a marker to copy the food pyramid (page 71) onto butcher paper. Have students find pictures of foods in magazines, cut them out, and glue them onto the pyramid. Display the food pyramid on a wall.

3. Designate a point value for each food group on the pyramid. For example, the breads and cereals group can be worth five points; the fruits and vegetables group, four points; the milk group, three points; the meat group, two points; and the fats group, one point. Write the point value of each group on the pyramid.

4. Divide the class into two teams. Have teams choose a name and write it on the board. Give each team 20 points to with which to start. Then explain and model the rules of the game.
   a. One player from each team comes to the front of the room. The first player tosses a squishy ball at the pyramid. If the ball hits a section of the pyramid, that player's team has a chance to win points by answering a question.
   b. Ask a question from the **Pyramid of Fun: Questions and Answers reproducibles (pages 72–73)**. If the player answers the question correctly, his or her team wins points based on the point value of the food group (e.g., a question about the meat group is worth two points).
   c. If the player answers incorrectly, the team loses the same number of points. A player from another team may choose to answer the same question or throw the ball and answer a new question.
   d. The game continues with teams taking turns throwing the ball and answering questions. The game is over when all the questions have been answered or one team loses all of its points.

5. Play a practice round to make sure students understand how to play the game. Then invite them to begin.

6. After the game, have students name their favorite foods. Challenge them to identify the food groups to which these foods belong. Use this opportunity to initiate a discussion about healthy eating habits and the importance of exercise.

Extended Learning

Place index cards, markers, and science books at a center. Invite students to write their own questions and answers for the current science topic they are studying. Use these cards to play a new round of Pyramid of Fun.

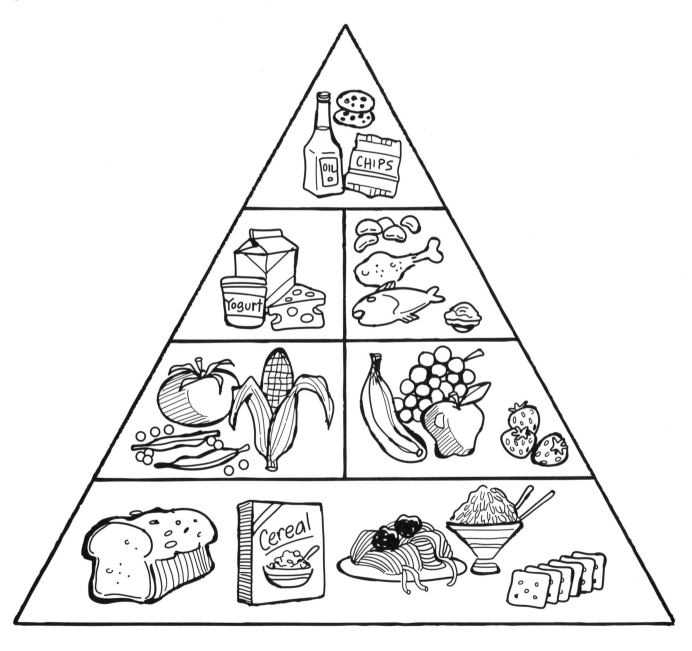

Pyramid of Fun: Questions and Answers

Skeletal System

Q: What holds up your body and gives it shape?
A: *Your skeleton holds up your body and gives it shape.*

Q: What do bones do?
A: *Some bones help you move, and some protect parts inside your body.*

Q: Which bone protects your brain?
A: *Your skull protects your brain.*

Q: Which bones protect your heart?
A: *Your rib bones protect your heart.*

Q: What other organ do your rib bones protect?
A: *Your rib bones protect your lungs.*

Muscular System

Q: What do muscles do?
A: *Some muscles work to move bones. Some have other jobs.*

Q: What does the heart muscle do?
A: *The heart pumps blood through the body.*

Q: What muscles help you to jump?
A: *Your leg muscles help you to jump.*

Q: How can you keep your bones and muscles healthy?
A: *You can exercise and eat healthy food.*

Q: Which food group includes food that helps bones stay healthy and strong?
A: *The milk group has food that helps bones stay healthy and strong.*

Respiratory System

Q: What do lungs do?
A: *Lungs help you get the oxygen you need from the air you breathe.*

Q: How many lungs do you have?
A: *You have two lungs.*

Q: When you breathe in, do your lungs get larger or smaller?
A: *When you breathe in, your lungs get larger.*

Q: Which part of the respiratory system is outside of your body?
A: *Your nose is outside of your body.*

Q: Which two openings bring in air to your lungs?
A: *The nose and mouth bring in air to your lungs.*

Pyramid of Fun: Questions and Answers

Circulatory System

Q: How many hearts do you have?
A: *You have one heart.*

Q: Why is exercise good for your heart and lungs?
A: *When you exercise, your heart and lungs work harder and get stronger.*

Q: Does your heart rate go faster or slower when you exercise?
A: *When you exercise, your heart rate goes faster.*

Q: What small tubes carry blood to different parts of your body?
A: *Veins carry blood to different parts of your body.*

Q: How many chambers are in your heart?
A: *There are four chambers in your heart.*

Digestive System

Q: What does your body digest to get energy and nutrients?
A: *Your body digests food to get energy and nutrients.*

Q: What does *digest* mean?
A: *Digest means to break down food.*

Q: What is in your mouth that helps digest food?
A: *Saliva in your mouth helps to digest food.*

Q: Where does food go after it leaves your mouth?
A: *It goes down a tube called the esophagus.*

Q: Where does the esophagus tube go?
A: *The tube goes into your stomach.*

Q: What does your stomach do?
A: *Your stomach squeezes food and mixes it with juices that digest it.*

Q: Where does the food go after it leaves the stomach?
A: *Food goes into the small intestine after it leaves the stomach.*

Q: What carries nutrients to all parts of your body?
A: *Your blood carries nutrients to all parts of your body.*

Q: Where does food go that your body does not use?
A: *Food that your body does not use goes to the large intestine.*

CHAPTER 4

Social Studies

May I Ride in Your Boat?

Materials
- Transportation Pictures reproducible
- Transportation Grid Map reproducible
- scissors
- glue
- crayons
- small envelopes
- thin red and green markers

Objective
Students will practice using grid maps while reviewing modes of transportation.

Understanding simple letter–number grid systems is a standard of learning for second graders. Students learn that lines that form squares divide a grid map. The grid map is labeled, so students can easily find designated locations. This engaging grid game gives students the opportunity to practice this essential skill while reinforcing important social studies concepts.

1. Ask students to name all the different types of transportation they have taken (e.g., *train, airplane, car, bus, truck, helicopter, hot-air balloon, boat*). Then tell them they will be playing a game in which they try to find and "capture" their partner's vehicles.

2. Give each student a set of cards cut from the **Transportation Pictures reproducible (page 76)**. Invite students to color and write their name on the back of the "For the Envelope" pictures, and then place these pictures in an envelope. Have them color and set aside the "For the Grid" pictures.

3. Give each student two copies of the **Transportation Grid Map reproducible (page 77)**. Have students glue the "For the Grid" pictures onto one of the grid maps. Show them how to match the dots on each picture with an intersecting grid line. Let the grid maps dry before students play the game. They will need the other grid map to mark the locations of their partner's vehicles.

4. Divide the class into pairs, and have pairs sit back-to-back so they cannot see each other's papers. Have students take out their grid maps and envelope of pictures. Give each student a red marker and a green marker. Then invite a volunteer to play the game with you while you explain the rules. The object of the game is for each player to identify the location of his or her opponent's vehicles.
   a. Player 1 asks, for example: *May I ride in your train?* Player 2 responds: *Sure, if you can find it!*

b. Player 1 gives a grid location (e.g., *Is it on A-5?*). If one of the train's dots is on A-5, player 2 responds *yes.*

c. If Player 2 says *yes,* Player 1 uses the green marker to draw a small *X* on A-5 on his or her grid map. (This is the map players use to monitor the locations of their partner's vehicles.) Player 2 also draws a green *X* on the dot on his or her train. These markings show both players that part of the train has been found.

d. If Player 1 names a grid location and Player 2 says *no,* Player 1 marks that location with a red *X.* Player 2 does not need to mark anything on his or her grid map.

e. If there is a different vehicle on a grid location other than the one Player 1 requested, Player 2 replies: *No, my train is not there. Would you like to ride on my bus?* This lets Player 1 know that he or she found Player 2's bus and not the train. Players draw a green *X* on their grid maps for the bus.

f. Play continues with partners taking turns naming grid locations. When a player names the grid locations for an entire vehicle, his or her partner must hand over the picture of that vehicle from the envelope. The first player with all of his or her partner's vehicles wins the game!

5. As you model the game with a volunteer, ask students to identify the locations on the grid map and tell if you have located your partner's vehicle. Ask them which color marker you should use to mark the grid map. Once students have a good understanding of the game, allow them to play independently.

6. As a follow-up, ask students to think of and draw several other categories of pictures to use for future games, such as mammals, flowers, toys, clothing, and so on.

Transportation Pictures

FOR THE GRID

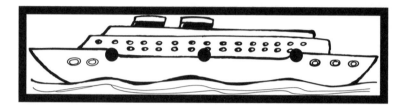

FOR THE ENVELOPE

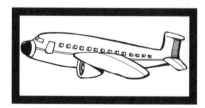

Reproducible

Name _____ Date _____

Transportation Grid Map

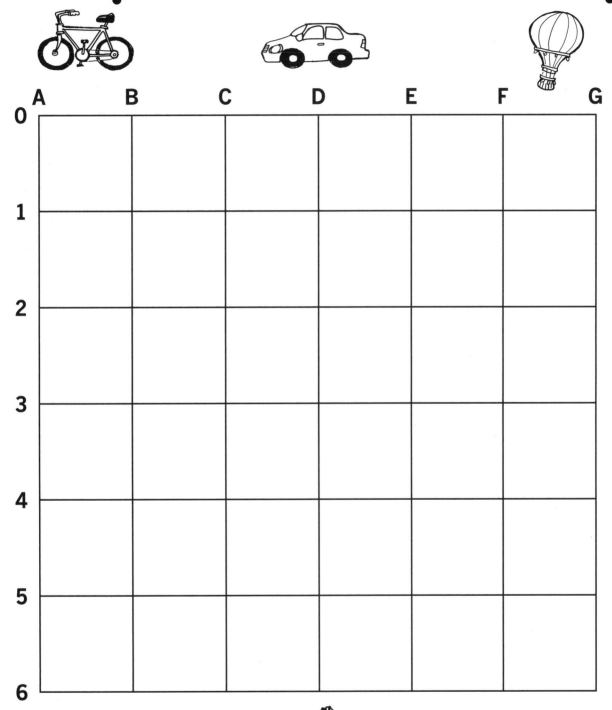

978-1-4129-5931-5 • © Corwin Press

Reproducible

Tic-Tac-Toe Bingo

Materials

- Tic-Tac-Toe Bingo Card reproducible
- drawing paper
- index cards
- game markers (e.g., small paper squares, pennies)

Objective

Students will match geography vocabulary words with their definitions.

Combining two great children's games, Tic-Tac-Toe and Bingo, will give students an easy and fun way to learn the names and meanings of geography terms. Second graders must be able to identify geographic features such as oceans, mountains, and lakes on a map. This game offers a brain-friendly opportunity to practice and reinforce learning!

1. Spark students' interest by asking them to draw the following: lake, river, mountain, plain, valley, peninsula, canyon, hill, island, and ocean. Do they recognize each geographic feature? Next, ask students to provide the meanings of the terms. Are they able to define them? If they can, then this game will be an easy way for students to show off their knowledge. If they cannot, then this game will help them learn the definitions.

2. Give students a double-sided copy of the **Tic-Tac-Toe Bingo Card reproducible (page 80)**. Have them choose nine of the geographic words from the box and write them on the game card, one word in each box. Have students prepare a second game card on the back of the reproducible.

3. Prepare geography vocabulary cards by writing the words and definitions on index cards. (See the box below.)

Geographic Words and Definitions

canyon: very deep valley

hill: land that is higher than the land around it but lower than a mountain

island: land that has water all around it

lake: body of water with land all around it

mountain: highest kind of land

ocean: very large body of salt water

peninsula: land that has water on three sides

plain: flat land

river: long body of water that flows across the land

valley: low land between hills or mountains

---

4. Give each student several game markers. Explain and model the rules of the game.

    a. Read aloud a definition from one of the index cards.

    b. Players identify the geography word that matches the definition and place a marker on the word on their game card.

    c. The first player to place three markers in a row (horizontally, vertically, or diagonally) calls out: *Tic-Tac-Toe Bingo!* Check the player's game card to verify he or she has covered all the correct words.

    d. Players then remove their markers, and a new game begins.

5. Play a practice round to check students' understanding. Then begin a real game. Play several rounds to reinforce learning.

6. As a follow-up, test students' ability to define the words. Chances are, students' memories will be much improved!

Extended Learning

This game makes a great center activity. Adapt the Tic-Tac-Toe Bingo Card so students can practice vocabulary in other content areas. Type a new set of words on a small piece of paper and tape it over the word box. Make copies of the new game card, and make definition cards to match the new words.

Tic-Tac-Toe Bingo Card

Directions: Choose nine words from the box. Write one word in each box of the game card.

river	ocean	mountain	canyon	peninsula
lake	hill	valley	plain	island

Needs and Wants Around the World

Objective
Students will understand and differentiate between needs and wants.

Materials
• index cards

Students love to play Around the World! In this version of the game, students compete to determine whether or not a card describes a want or a need.

1. Ahead of time, write on index cards various needs and wants. Label the back of each card *want* or *need*. Use the following suggestions as a guide. Needs: *food, water, fresh air, shelter, love, medicine.* Wants: *chocolate milkshake, skates, tickets, books, juicy steak.*

2. Get students warmed up for the game by asking: *Who needs a million dollars? Will you die if you do not get it?* Explain that they do not really need it. Have students talk about things they want versus things they need. Guide them to explain how a want is different than a need. (A *want* describes something we would like to have. A *need* describes something we must have in order to live a healthy life.)

3. Have the class sit in a circle. Tell students they will play a game to demonstrate their understanding of wants and needs. Explain and model the rules of the game.
   a. Choose a player to stand behind someone in the circle. Read aloud a game card.
   b. The two players try to be the first to identify whether the card describes a want or a need. Other students should not help them or shout out the answer.
   c. When the standing player answers correctly, he or she stands behind the next student sitting in the circle. If the player gets "around the world" (the circle), he or she wins the game. If the player answers incorrectly, he or she sits in the place of the seated student, who then stands up to compete against the next seated student.

4. Invite students to play the game. Make sure they play politely without giving clues to their classmates.

5. As a follow-up, have students share one need and one want related to the classroom or their school.

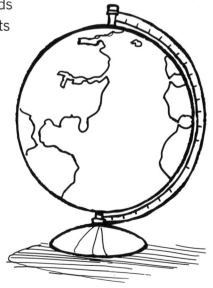

"Memory from Afar" Matching Game

Objective

Students will learn about special Americans from long ago.

Students in second grade learn about historical figures who have helped their country, their state, their community, or others in a special way. Help students remember important figures by having them play the game *Memory from Afar*.

Materials
- construction paper
- beanbag

1. Ahead of time, use a marker to write names of historical figures and clues to their identities on separate pieces of construction paper. For example, write *Sojourner Truth* on one piece of paper and *A woman who fought against slavery* on another.

2. Get students' brains focused by asking: *Who is the governor of our state?* Toss a beanbag to a student. Continue asking these types of questions as students toss around the beanbag. Tell students they will play a matching game that features special Americans from the past.

3. Divide the class into two teams. Have two students act as "card flippers." Place the construction paper "cards" facedown in a grid pattern on the floor. Then explain and model the rules of the game.

   a. A player from the first team tosses the beanbag onto one of the cards. A card flipper turns over the card. Everyone reads the card.

   b. The player then tosses the beanbag onto another card. The card flipper turns over that card for everyone to read.

   c. If the two cards match (an historical figure with the matching clue), the team takes both cards and sends another player to take a turn. If the cards do not match, the card flippers turn both cards facedown again, and a player from the other team takes a turn.

   d. Play continues until all the cards have been matched. The team with the most sets of matching cards wins the game!

4. Remind students that the game challenges them in two ways—to match people and their descriptions, and to remember where previously flipped cards are located for later matches. Then mix up the cards again to begin the game.

5. As a follow-up, have students suggest and create cards of other historical figures for the game.

First, Next, Last

Objective

Students will practice sequencing events while creating timelines that cover various social studies topics.

Materials
- white construction paper
- crayons or markers

Students need to understand that events occur in a sequence. They get lots of practice identifying the beginning, middle, and ending of stories. They should continue this exercise in social studies. Timelines are the social studies' way of teaching sequence. In this game, students will sequence events on a timeline.

1. Get students' brains ready for sequencing by telling a simple story, but tell the events of the story out of order. You will get some confused looks! Stress the importance of telling events in their order of occurrence. Invite students to help you put the events in the correct order, and then retell the story.

2. Create a list of events to sequence based on social studies lessons. Events might include the following: how milk gets from a cow to the students' dinner table, the major events in the life of a famous American, or the development of the American flag from the time of the colonies to the present.

3. Divide the class into groups of four. Give each student a piece of white construction paper and crayons or markers. Have students fold their paper in half. Explain that these papers will serve as cards for a sequencing game.

4. Then model the game as you explain the rules to students.
   a. Assign each team an event to sequence. Teams must sequence the event in four steps. Players should think about the words *first, next, then,* and *last* as they organize their thoughts.
   b. Each team member writes a sentence and draws a picture on one side of his or her "card" to illustrate one step of the event.
   c. Collect all the cards and mix them up as players sit together on the carpet. Give each player a card.
   d. Players then walk around the room, searching for classmates who have the cards that go with their event. When players find their partners, they work together to sequence the cards and then place them upright on desks or tables.
   e. Each group of students who originally made the cards must then describe the events they illustrated.

5. Name an event, and ask students to break it down into four steps. Record their responses. Ask volunteers to describe pictures you could draw to represent the steps. Answer any questions, and then begin the game.

6. After the game, discuss why it was important to use the words *first*, *next*, *then*, and *last*. Discuss how not using those words would make sequencing the events much more difficult.

Extended Learning

Have students use the sentences and drawings from the game to write short paragraphs. Invite them to choose an event to write about and think of a main idea sentence that introduces the events. Encourage students to use the game cards to help them organize their paragraph. Remind them to add interesting descriptions and details to their writing.

First, the farmer milks the cow.

Then, the truck driver takes the milk to the bottling factory.

Next, the truck driver takes the milk cartons to the store.

Last, your parents buy the milk and bring it home.

The Name Game

Objective

Students will review facts from social studies lessons.

Materials
• none

Once in a while, there are a few extra minutes available in class (such as after an assembly). There is no time to start something new but too much time to do nothing. Use this game to apply those extra minutes in the pursuit of reviewing or rehearsing previously learned information.

1. Get students' attention by singing or chanting a rhyme. Begin by slapping your thighs and then clapping your hands to create a steady 1-2-3-4 beat. Tell students that they will review facts from social studies lessons with a fun chanting game.

2. On the beat, chant the following: *I can name a state in America. Can (student's name)?* The student responds, slapping thighs and clapping hands on the beat: *Yes, I can!* (or, *Ask me later!*)

   Continue: *Tell me now,* or *Can (another student's name)?* The student responds, for example: *Nevada is a state in America.*

   Nod "yes," then continue: *Who else can name a state in America? Can (student's name)?*

   Continue the chant, eventually calling again on the students who said: *Ask me later.*

3. Chant anything you have taught that you need to review. For example: *I can name the bodies of water on the earth, names of presidents, earth's natural resources, what people need to survive,* or *Native American tribes.*

4. After the game, invite a volunteer to make a list of the answers on chart paper so students can observe what they know. The visual reminder will also give students who are insecure in their knowledge another opportunity to learn.

Florida is a state in America!

CHAPTER 5

Physical Education, Art, and Music

Animal Acrobats

Materials
• long jump ropes

Objective

Students will explore various ways of moving their bodies from one location to another.

Second graders should continue to improve the development of skills in running, jumping, leaping, twisting, galloping, crawling, hopping, and skipping. Give students a great cardio workout as well as a chance to improve their movement skills with a game of Animal Acrobats.

1. Generate interest in the game by asking students to show how a frog moves. Repeat with other animals such as a kangaroo and a rabbit. Ask students to discuss how these animals' movements are different. Then ask them if they can run fast, like a cheetah. Take students outdoors for a test run.

2. Tell students they will be animal acrobats as they compete in a relay race. Divide the class into five teams. Place one or two jump ropes on the ground to make a starting line. Have teams line up single-file behind the line. Use jump ropes to create a second line about 30 feet away.

3. Explain and model the rules of the game.
   a. One player from each team stands on the starting line.
   b. Call out: *On your mark, get set, move like a gorilla!* Players move like a gorilla to the next jump-rope line and then return.
   c. Players tag the hand of the next teammate, and the game continues until all players have completed the race. The team that finishes first wins!
   d. Begin a new race by naming a new animal, or invite players to name animals.

4. Have teams play a practice round, and then begin the race.

5. As a follow-up, have students discuss which animal movements were the easiest and which were the most difficult. Invite them to talk about how the way different animals move might help them survive in their environments.

Fearsome Threesomes

Objective

Students will practice the skills of kicking, jumping, throwing, and catching.

Materials
• soccer balls

Second graders enjoy playing in small groups. Give them an opportunity to develop their skills in kicking, jumping, throwing, and catching while they develop their understanding and respect for each other's differences in physical abilities. Grouped in clusters of three, they will become fearsome threesomes in their physical prowess!

1. Ask students to tell what muscles they use when jumping, kicking, and throwing and catching a ball. Invite a volunteer to pantomime each activity and have the class note which muscles are engaged. Focus students' attention on how the arms lift up when jumping; how one leg balances the body while the other one kicks; how the waist, shoulders, and hips are involved in throwing; and how knees bend to absorb the shock of catching a ball. Ask all students to practice the motions to make them more aware of how their bodies are moving.

2. Take the class outside. Tell students they will use their muscles as they compete in three different games. Divide the class into teams of three. Give each team a soccer ball. Then demonstrate how to play each game with a group of volunteers.

   Game 1: For the first game, team members stand in a triangle formation. Students must kick the soccer ball from one player to another, without the ball escaping the triangle area. Players use their bodies and feet to trap and control the ball before they kick it.

   Game 2: Teams practice throwing and catching the ball. While still standing in a triangular formation, they demonstrate the following types of throwing: overhead pass, two-arm underhand pass, two-arm thrust, and one-arm throw.

Game 3: For the third game, team members stand in a row. The players on the ends roll the ball to each other as quickly as possible. The player in the middle must jump over the ball. Players on the ends must take care to roll the ball smoothly on the ground. No bouncing balls are allowed! When the middle player has jumped over the ball five times, a new player moves to the middle spot and the game continues.

3. Answer any questions, and then have students play independently. Circulate around the groups to monitor students and ensure they are following the rules.

4. As a follow-up, ask students to describe how their muscles feel. Prompt students with questions such as: *Did you use the muscles you thought you would? Which exercise was the easiest? Which one was the most difficult?* Discuss with students the ways they may have adjusted their play based on their classmates' abilities. Did some of them have to work harder to keep up with their partners? Did some of them have to play more gently to accommodate another player?

Extended Learning

Invite the Fearsome Threesomes to try different activities. For example, have them practice shooting baskets at the basketball court. The first player shoots the ball, the second player grabs the rebound and shoots, and the third player runs up to grab that rebound and then shoots. Teams may also compete in a handball relay. Have each threesome line up at the back of a handball court. The first player hits a rubber ball against the handball wall and then runs to the end of the line. The second and third players repeat these actions.

978-1-4129-5931-5

Mirror, Mirror

Objective

Students will observe and copy movements made by their partners.

Materials
- game materials (e.g., beanbags, jump ropes, hula hoops, balls)

Students can increase their powers of observation and concentration by watching another classmate do an activity, and then trying to exactly mirror that activity. Invite students to use their creativity to play the game *Mirror, Mirror*.

1. Ask students if they have ever said or heard someone say for example: *"So-and-so" is copying me!* (Be sure to say it in a whiny voice!) Tell students that today you want them to copy each other as they play a new game.

2. Take the class to an outdoor play area. Place the game materials around the play area so students are free to get them as needed. Divide the class into pairs.

3. Tell students that they will take turns copying exactly what their partner is doing. Ask them to imagine that they are looking in a mirror and must "reflect" exactly their partner's actions. Invite a volunteer to model the game as you explain the rules.

   a. One player says: *Mirror, mirror, on the wall, can you do "this" at all?* The player grabs an item and performs a movement with it. (For example, a player might pick up a beanbag, toss it in the air, and catch it.)
   b. His or her partner must mirror the action as closely as possible.
   c. Players then switch roles and play again.

4. Point out the objects for the game, and invite students to name possible mirror actions they could perform with them. Then have students play on their own. Encourage students to use their creativity, and assist them with their movements as needed.

5. After the game, have partners demonstrate their favorite mirror movements for the rest of the class.

Wings of Symmetry

Materials

- Butterfly Pattern reproducible
- 2 apples
- knife
- construction paper
- scissors
- tempera paint
- cotton swabs

Objective

Students will explore the concept of symmetry and how it creates visual balance.

Symmetry can be defined as "being exactly the same on both sides of a central line." It is also defined as "the harmony or beauty of form that results from balanced proportions." In this game, students will enjoy exploring both of these artistic concepts.

1. Introduce the concept of symmetry by cutting an apple in half lengthwise. Point out to students that the two halves match, or are the same. Next, cut an apple across its width. Note that the top half does not match the bottom half. Invite students to discuss the differences.

2. Give each student a construction paper copy of the **Butterfly Pattern reproducible (page 91)**. Have students cut out the butterfly and then print their name in small letters on the back of both wings. Show them how to dip a cotton swab in paint and dot paint onto one side of the butterfly. Model how to fold the butterfly down the center and press the wings together. Invite students to pull the wings apart to observe the identical patterns on each wing.

3. Let the butterflies dry. Then have students cut down the center of their butterfly, creating two identical halves.

4. Divide the class into small groups. Collect the butterfly halves for each group and place them, painted side up, on a table. Have students work together to find the symmetrical wings and put the butterflies back together, as in a puzzle. They can check accuracy by matching the student names on the backs of the wings. Have groups trade pieces and play again.

5. After the game, have students discuss examples of symmetry they see in the world around them.

978-1-4129-5931-5

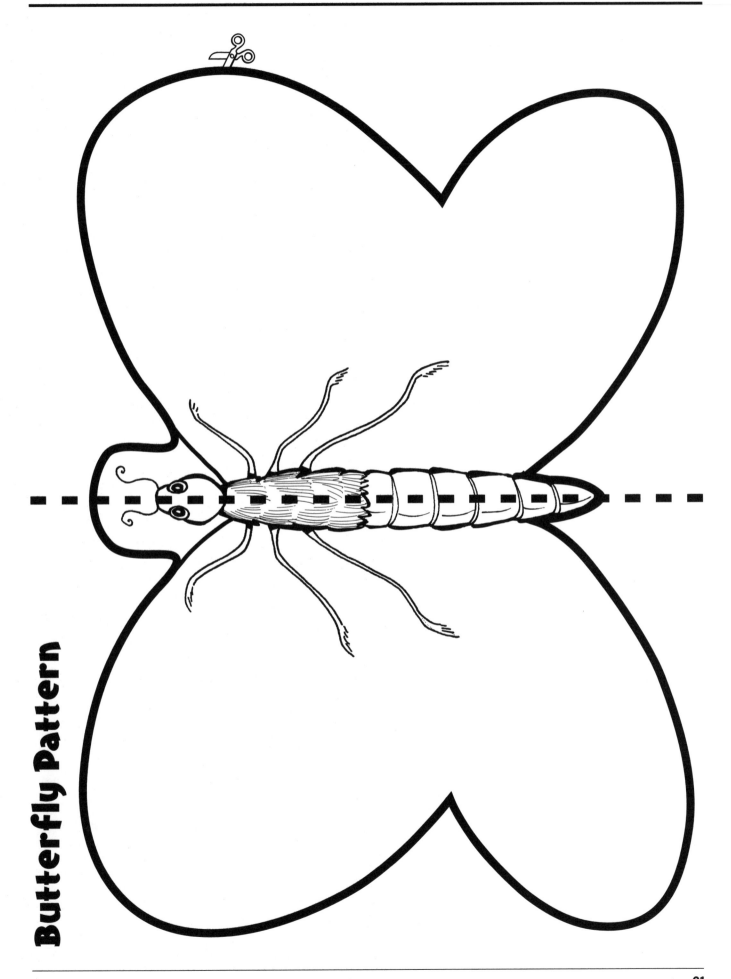

Butterfly Pattern

Picture This!

Materials
- magazines
- scissors
- magnets
- 2 cookie sheets

Objective

Students will use pictures to connect elements of art to other content areas across the curriculum.

In the national standards for visual arts, students are to use what they have learned and apply it to other situations. Have students practice this skill with a game of Picture This! In this game, students analyze and choose magazine pictures to illustrate concepts from other areas of knowledge.

1. Ask students to flip through magazines and cut out pictures of happy people. Gather all the pictures, and then ask students to explain how they knew the people in the pictures were happy. Focus on the upward, curved lines of smiles; the shining qualities of the eyes; and the unfurrowed lines of the brows.

2. Explain that we see principles of art in everyday life. For example, when a man turns a warm shade of red, it means he is probably embarrassed or angry. When a child's lips turn the cool shade of blue, it means she is very cold. The downward angle of a teacher's eyebrows may mean she is bothered by something.

3. Invite students to explore the elements of art in everyday objects and people. Have them cut out several pictures, including people, objects, and animals.

4. Have students place the pictures faceup on a large table. Place two cookie sheets and magnets on the table. Divide the class into two teams. Tell students they will use the pictures to play a game. Then explain and model the rules of the game.
   a. Each team sends two players to the picture table.
   b. Name a concept the players will show by using the pictures. (See Ideas for Concepts on the following page.)
   c. Players take the pictures they need and use magnets to stick them on the cookie sheets. The first player to do so accurately scores a point for his or her team, as long as that player can also explain the concept.
   d. Play for a set amount of time. The team with the most points wins the game.

Ideas for Concepts

Opposites	Love
Happiness	Excitement
Fear	Frustration
Symmetry	Past, Present, Future
Multiplication, Division	Things Grow and Change
Subtraction, Addition	Technology
Warmth	Isolation
Coolness	Togetherness
Anger	Surprise

5. Play a practice round. Have two volunteers come to the table. Give them the concept *opposites*. Ask the class to help the students identify pictures that illustrate the concept. For example, they might find pictures of a large dog and a small dog or pictures of a black purse and a white purse. Ask students to explain why each pair of pictures illustrates the concept of opposites. Answer any questions, and then begin the game.

6. As a follow-up, discuss with students what was easy or difficult about the game. Prompt students with questions such as: *Was it better to work with a partner, or would it have been easier to find pictures by yourself? Were some concepts easier or more difficult than others to show? Why? How did knowing about the elements of art (e.g., line, color, texture, size, mood, space) help you choose pictures?*

Extended Learning

Have students use pictures from the game to make charts that illustrate the various concepts. Print concepts on separate pieces of chart paper, and have students glue the pictures on the corresponding papers. Encourage them to write the names of the items and descriptive adjectives to help English language learners develop their vocabulary.

Recycled Band

Objective

Students will create a rhythmic pattern using recycled materials.

Materials
- rhythmic music on CD or cassette
- CD or cassette player
- Lummi sticks or pieces of dowel cut into 12" lengths
- empty, clean soda cans
- empty, clean milk jugs

Keeping a steady beat is an important skill for students to develop. Keeping a beat develops their listening skills and their abilities in one-to-one correspondence. This activity allows students to work together as "pieces" to become part of a "whole." They must pay attention to the beat while they play a "gig" as the Recycled Band!

1. Students love to clap their hands to music. Get them into their musical selves by playing some music and inviting them to dance and clap to the beat. Invite students who love to dance (and enjoy performing) to enter the middle of the circle and teach everyone a new step or two!

2. Tell students they will work in small groups to create a band. Explain that they must listen carefully if they want to earn points for their group. Divide the class into three groups.

3. Explain that you will pass out the "band instruments" that they will use in the game. Remind them to hold the instruments quietly until you give them instructions. Give each student in Group 1 two Lummi sticks. Give each student in Group 2 one Lummi stick and an empty soda can. Give each student in Group 3 one Lummi stick and an empty milk jug.

4. During the game, students will make music as the Recycled Band. Explain that group members will play their instruments on different counts of a four-count beat. Group 1 will play their Lummi sticks on every beat: *1-2-3-4*. Group 2 will hit their Lummi sticks against the soda cans on the second and fourth beats: *1-2-3-4*. Group 3 will hit their Lummi sticks against the milk jugs on the first and third beats: *1-2-3-4*.

5. Give groups time to practice with their instruments. Teach students the word *dynamics*, which is how loudly or how quietly they should play. As students explore their instruments, pay attention to which group needs to play more loudly or softly. Tell students how you would like them to play, and award points to groups as they follow instructions. Remind students that although they are in separate groups, they are working together as one big band. Then begin the concert!

6. Get your band's attention. Tap your own Lummi stick and raise it like a conductor's baton. Give students a steady 1-2-3-4 beat, and then point to Group 1. They start to play: **1-2-3-4, 1-2-3-4, 1-2-3-4**. Then point to Group 2. They join in: *1-2-3-4, 1-2-3-4, 1-2-3-4*. Next, point to Group 3. They join in: **1**-2-**3**-4, **1**-2-**3**-4, **1**-2-**3**-4.

7. Keep the music going, and then change the dynamics. Tell one group to play more loudly and another to play more softly. Then tell all groups to play loudly and then softly. Stop Group 3, and then stop Group 2, and finally, stop Group 1, so the music ends on the fourth beat.

8. Award points to groups for following instructions. Hopefully, all three groups will tie and the whole band is declared as the winner! Award students with small treats, such as pencils or stickers, for performing an entertaining concert.

9. After the game, use the band instruments to discuss recycling. Have students explore using different recycled instruments (e.g., hitting a Lummi stick against a basketball, hitting the soda can on the milk jug, or a tapping pencil against a book).

Extended Learning

Have the class sing "Hot Cross Buns" as the band plays. Or, invite a volunteer to be the band singer and come to the front of the classroom to sing as the band plays.

References

Banks, J. A., Beyer, B. K., Contreras, G., & Craven, J. (1999). *People together: Adventures in time and place.* New York, NY: McGraw-Hill School Division.

Beyers, J. (1998). The biology of human play. *Child Development, 69*(3), 599–600.

Bjorkland, D. F., & Brown, R. D. (1998). Physical play and cognitive development: Integrating activity, cognition, and education. *Child Development, 69*(3), 604–606.

Education World. (1996–2007). *National education standards.* Retrieved April 3, 2007, from http://www. education-world.com/standards/.

Gardner, H. (1983). *Frames of mind: The theory of multiple intelligences.* New York, NY: Basic Books.

Harcourt science, California edition, grade 2. (2000). Orlando, FL: Harcourt School Publishers.

Jensen, E. (1995). *Brain-based learning and teaching.* Del Mar, CA: The Brain Store.

Jensen, E. (2001). *Arts with the brain in mind.* Alexandria, VA: Association for Supervision and Curriculum Development.

McCarthy, B. (1990). Using the 4MAT system to bring learning styles to schools. *Educational Leadership, 48*(2), 31–37.

National Council for the Social Studies. (2002). *Expectations of excellence: Curriculum standards for social studies.* Silver Spring, MD: National Council for the Social Studies (NCSS).

National Council of Teachers of English and the International Reading Association. (1996). *Standards for the English language arts.* Urbana, IL: National Council of Teachers of English (NCTE).

National Council of Teachers of Mathematics. (2005). *Principles and standards for school mathematics.* Reston, VA: National Council of Teachers of Mathematics (NCTM).

National Research Council. (1996). *National science education standards.* Washington, DC: National Academy Press.

Tate, M. L. (2003). *Worksheets don't grow dendrites: 20 instructional strategies that engage the brain.* Thousand Oaks, CA: Corwin Press.

Time4Learning. (2003–2007). *Second grade word lists.* Retrieved March 10, 2007, from http://www. time4learning.com/SpellingWords/2nd-grade-spelling-words.shtml.

Wolfe, P. (2001). *Brain matters: Translating research into classroom practice.* Alexandria, VA: Association for Supervision and Curriculum Development.